Daily Devotions for Die-Hard Kids

TO PARENTS/GUARDIANS FROM THE AUTHOR

DAILY DEVOTIONS FOR DIE-HARD KIDS is an adaptation of our DAILY DEVOTIONS FOR DIE-HARD FANS series. It is suggested for children ages 6 to 12, but that guideline is, of course, flexible. Only the parents or other adults can appraise the spiritual maturity of their children.

The devotions are written with the idea that a parent or adult will join the children to act as a mentor and spiritual guide for each devotion and the discussion that may ensue. The devotions seek to engage the child by capitalizing on his or her interest in the particular collegiate team the family follows. The interest in college sports is thus an oblique and somewhat tricky way, if you will, to lead your children to reading the Bible and learning about God, Jesus, and faith.

Each devotion contains a short Bible reading (except for occasional longer stories that must be read in their entirety), a paraphrase of the most pertinent scripture verse, a true A&M sports story, and a theological discussion that ties everything together through a common theme. The devotion then concludes with a suggested activity that is based on the theme of the day. I tie each day's theological message to a child's life by referring to such aspects as school, household chores, video games, and relations with parents, siblings, and teachers, etc.

The devotions are intended to be fun for both the adult and the child, but they are also intended to be attempts to spark interest in quite serious matters of faith and living a godly life. A point of emphasis throughout the book is to impress upon the child that faith is not just for the times when the family gathers for formal worship in a particular structure, but rather is for every moment of every day wherever he or she may be.

Our children are under attack by the secular world as never before. It is a time fraught with danger for the innocence and the faith of our most precious family members. I pray that this book will provide your children with a better understanding of what it means to be a Christian. I also pray that this book will help lay the foundation for what will be a lifelong journey of faith for your children. May God bless you and your family.

ED MCMINN

Daily Devotions for Die-Hard Kids: Texas Longhorns
© 2016, 2022 Ed McMinn; Extra Point Publishers; P.O. Box 6405;
Christiansburg VA 24068

DAILY DEVOTIONS FOR DIE-HARD FANS

ACC
CLEMSON TIGERS
DUKE BLUE DEVILS
FSU SEMINOLES
GA. TECH YELLOW JACKETS
NORTH CAROLINA TAR HEELS
NC STATE WOLFPACK
NOTRE DAME FIGHTING IRISH
VIRGINIA CAVALIERS
VIRGINIA TECH HOKIES

BIG 10
MICHIGAN WOLVERINES
MICHIGAN STATE SPARTANS
NEBRASKA CORNHUSKERS
OHIO STATE BUCKEYES
PENN STATE NITTANY LIONS

BIG 12
BAYLOR BEARS
OKLAHOMA SOONERS
OKLAHOMA STATE COWBOYS
TEXAS LONGHORNS
TEXAS TECH RED RAIDERS
WEST VIRGINIA MOUNTAINEERS

INDEPENDENT
NOTRE DAME FIGHTING IRISH

SEC
ALABAMA CRIMSON TIDE
MORE ALABAMA CRIMSON TIDE
ARKANSAS RAZORBACKS
AUBURN TIGERS
MORE AUBURN TIGERS
FLORIDA GATORS
GEORGIA BULLDOGS
MORE GEORGIA BULLDOGS
KENTUCKY WILDCATS
LSU TIGERS
MISSISSIPPI STATE BULLDOGS
MISSOURI TIGERS
OLE MISS REBELS
SOUTH CAROLINA GAMECOCKS
TEXAS A&M AGGIES
TENNESSEE VOLUNTEERS

AND NASCAR

DAILY DEVOTIONS FOR DIE-HARD KIDS

ALABAMA; AUBURN; BAYLOR; GEORGIA; LSU; MISS. STATE;
OLE MISS; TENNESSEE; TEXAS; TEXAS A&M

IN THE BEGINNING

Read Genesis 1:1; 2:1-3.

In the beginning, God created the heavens and the earth.

The ball exploded during the first scrimmage. Other than that little problem, Texas football got off to a good beginning.

Three Texas students who had played some football organized the first-ever UT football squad in 1893. They held some daily practices and then played an intrasquad game. (That's a game with the Texas players divided into two teams, kind of like PE.)

Early in the game, one of the players was tackled and fell on the ball. It promptly blew apart. Everyone had to sit around for about thirty minutes while a student got a horse and rode to town to fetch a new football.

The first official game for the new university team was against the "Dallas Foot Ball Club."

The Texas boys made a nine-hour train trip to Dallas for the game. They missed dinner when the horse-drawn rig showed up early at the hotel to take them to the game.

Texas' team scored the first time it had the ball to lead 4-0. Texas would never trail. The final score was an 18-16 university win.

Football at UT had begun.

Beginnings are important, but how we use those beginnings is even more important. You get a new beginning in your life every time the sun comes up and brings you a new day.

Have you ever thought that every morning is a gift from God? Well, it is. This present of a new day shows God's love for you. Each new day is full of promise. You can use it to make some wrong things right and to do some good.

How you use your new day is up to you. You should just make sure you walk with God all day long.

Try starting each morning by thanking God for the day and asking him to protect and lead you all day long.

CELEBRATION TIME

Read Luke 15:8-10.

*Heaven celebrates every time a
sinner turns away from his sin.*

Somebody hit the Texas pitcher right in his stomach. Another Longhorn was cleated in the face. It wasn't a fight. It was the celebration of a national championship.

On June 26, 2005, the Longhorns threw a big old dogpile after they swept Florida to win the school's sixth baseball national title. After J. Brent Cox struck out the last Gator batter, he dropped to his knees and pounded the dirt with both hands. Just as he stood up, UT catcher Taylor Teagarden plowed right into him. The pitcher and the catcher fell to the ground to start the dogpile.

Freshman catcher Todd Gilfillan came out of the pile looking like he had lost a fight. His face and his uniform had blood all over them.

The blood came from cuts over his right eye and on his right cheek. A teammate's cleats had had a close encounter with his face.

Gilfillan smiled about the whole thing. It was just part of the celebration. A little blood was a small price to pay for a national title.

Have you ever whooped and hollered when Texas scored a touchdown? Or maybe you just smiled and felt good inside the last time you got a hit in a softball or a baseball game.

When we're happy about something that just happened or something we did, we celebrate. We also celebrate special days, like your birthday or Easter Sunday.

Did you know God and the angels celebrate, too? They sing and shout and throw a party quite often. They celebrate every time someone accepts Jesus as their savior.

Just think. When you said "yes" to Jesus, you made the angels dance.

What did you do to celebrate your last birthday? Why does your family celebrate Christmas?

BLESS YOU

Read Ephesians 1:3-8.

In Jesus, God has blessed us with every spiritual blessing.

Laura Wilkinson regarded a broken foot as a blessing. How weird is that?

Wilkinson is one of the greatest divers in UT history. She won the national championship in both 1997 and 1999. She was inducted into the Longhorn Hall of Honor in 2009.

In March before the 2000 Olympics, Wilkinson broke a foot in three places during practice. A piece of bone floated to the bottom of her foot. It "felt like I was walking on a rock everywhere," she said.

So how in the world was that a blessing? She said the injury forced her to train harder.

She was in first place at the Olympics as she got ready for the dive she had been doing when she broke her foot. Her coach, Kenny Armstrong, told her, "Do it for Hilary." Hilary Grivich was Wilkinson's friend and teammate who had been killed in a car wreck.

Wilkinson recited her favorite Bible verse (Phil. 4:13), nailed the dive, and won the Gold Medal. A broken foot had helped her get ready.

Like Laura Wilkinson, you just never know where you will find blessings in life. At home, on the playground, in the classroom, at the swimming pool. Who knows?

What you can know is that God is always at work preparing blessings just for you. If you will trust in him and obey him, he will pour out those blessings on you.

While God wants only what is good for you, he doesn't manage a candy store. That means he won't bail you out when you make a bad decision or do something wrong. Instead, he will let you learn a lesson from your mistake.

But even that is a blessing. If you do learn, you'll never do it again. You'll be smarter. Even when you're crying, God blesses you.

Make a list of ten blessings in your life.

MAMA SAID

Read John 19:25-27.

Jesus' mother, Mary, stood near his cross.

She never worked a day for Texas. She never won any awards or honors from the school. But when she died in 2009, she was remembered as "one of the most important women in the history of Texas Longhorns football." She was Ann Campbell, who had a son named Earl.

Earl Campbell is a Longhorn legend, the winner of the 1977 Heisman Trophy. Many still consider him the greatest running back in state history.

College recruiters came from all over the country in 1974. They all had to go through Ann. She stood in the doorway and shooed any coaches away who made illegal offers. She said her son was not for sale.

The stress finally made her so sick she had

to go to bed. One night, a phone caller asked her if Oklahoma's head coach could come by. She raised up in bed "and looked Earl straight in the eye." "This has gone on long enough," she said. "You know you are going down to Texas with Coach [Darrell] Royal, so you tell them that."

Her son did what mama said. The rest is UT and collegiate football history.

Mamas do a lot for their kids, and they do it all out of love. Even when your mama tells you to do something you don't want to, she has a good reason. It's usually for your good.

Think about Jesus' mama for a minute. She loved her boy no matter what. When Mary stood near the cross, she was showing both love and courage. No matter how wrong it was, Jesus was condemned as an enemy of the Roman Empire. She could have been, too.

Love your mama like she loves you.

Make a list of the things your mama did for you today. Did you thank her? Do you thank God for her?

DAY 5

TICK TOCK

Matthew 25:1-13.

*Stay alert. You don't know the day
or the hour when Jesus will return.*

The clock ticked down to zero, but Texas still
had time to win the Big 12 championship.

In December 2009, the Longhorns and the
Nebraska Cornhuskers played a real thriller for
the league title. With only 1:44 left, Nebraska
kicked a field goal to lead 12-10.

Longhorn quarterback Colt McCoy led his
team down the field quickly. As the seconds
ticked away, McCoy took a snap and sailed the
ball out of bounds to stop the clock. To the
horror of UT fans, the clock ticked down to
0:00. The game was over — or so it seemed.

But McCoy was sure there was some time
left. He was right. The refs reviewed the play
and put one second back on the clock.

Senior Hunter Lawrence come on to try a
field goal. His holder, wide receiver Jordan

Shipley, shouted Jeremiah 17:7 to his kicker: "Blessed is the man who trusts in the Lord."

Lawrence's 46-yard kick was good. UT won 13-12. This time there really was no time left on the clock.

Even though you're a kid, the clock has a lot to do with your life. You have to be at school on time or you're headed for big trouble. Athletic events, classes, church, even birthday parties — they all start at a certain time. You probably have a bedtime on school nights.

All that time, every second of your life, is a gift from God since he's the one who dreamed up time in the first place.

So what does God consider making good use of the time he gives us? As Jesus' story tells us, it's being ready for the wonderful and glorious day when Jesus will return.

When will that be? Only time will tell.

Count to sixty but not real fast.
That's a minute. Any minute now
Jesus could come back.

DAY 6

MAKE NO MISTAKE

Read Mark 14:66-72.

*Peter remembered Jesus had said
to him, "Three times you will say
you don't know me." Peter cried.*

For two years, Bobby Layne remembered a mistake he had made. Then he got the chance to make people forget it.

A quarterback, Layne is a Longhorn legend. He left UT in 1947 with every passing record in school history. In 1944, Oklahoma State (then known as Oklahoma A&M) beat Layne and the Horns 13-8. Layne threw a bad pass in the game that led to an A&M score.

Layne went to a barber shop for a haircut a few days after the game. Talking about the loss, a Longhorn fan who didn't recognize the quarterback said Layne "just shouldn't have thrown the ball." Layne jumped up and said, "Listen, pal. You've had a whole weekend to think about this. If I had had that much time, I wouldn't have thrown the ball either."

Texas played an undefeated A&M team in 1946, and Layne got his revenge for his mistake in the '44 game. He scored four TDs, and Texas won 54-6.

Only one person has ever walked this Earth and been perfect. That was Jesus. You're not him. That means you will make mistakes. You will not make all hundreds on your tests. You will trip and fall sometimes and embarrass yourself. You will be mean to others sometime.

All your mistakes can be forgiven if you ask God for forgiveness. That means God forgets about them. Even Peter's awful mistake in denying that he knew Jesus was forgiven. He went on to be the main man in starting the Christian church.

The one mistake you must never make is to kick Jesus out of your life completely. God won't forget about that one.

**What mistakes did you make today
that hurt other people?
Ask God for forgiveness of them.**

VIRTUAL REALITY

Read Habakkuk 1:2-4.

*God, why do you put up with the
wrong things people are doing?*

On the field in front of 75,000 people, Texas' "Duke" Carlisle had his hand stuck down his pants. What in the world was he doing?

As a senior quarterback in 1962, Carlisle led the Horns to the championship of the Southwest Conference and the Cotton Bowl. In that bowl game, Carlisle seemed to behave in a way that he shouldn't have in front of a bunch of people.

During the game, he found a 50-cent piece on the field and stuck it in his pants. Later, he was in on a tackle and felt a sharp pain in his leg. The coin was being pushed into his flesh. He started kicking and screaming.

Back on his feet, Carlisle reached into his pants to get the coin. Instead, he pushed it farther down. "At about the 50-yard line in front of 75,000 people, I had my entire right arm jammed down my pants," Carlisle said.

A referee came over and asked, "You got a problem there, son?" Carlisle said he'd be OK in a minute. "I sure hope so," the ref said, "because that doesn't look real good."

You know, sometimes things just aren't what they seem. It's like a mirror in a fun house at the fair. Have you ever seen one of those? It makes you look all wacky and distorted.

It's that way with the world; it looks like nobody's in charge. We have wars everywhere. People hurt and kill other people. Children go to bed hungry at night. What's going on?

That's what Habakkuk asked God long ago, and God answered him. God said things aren't what they seem. He said he was in control and one day he would make everything all right.

We just have to trust and believe in God.

As Habakkuk did, name some things you'd like to see God change about this world. Pray for those changes.

DAY 8

SIZE MATTERS

Read Luke 19:1-10.

Zacchaeus wanted to see Jesus, but he was so short, he had to climb a tree.

Malcolm Kutner was so scrawny he had to beg the Texas coaches to let him play football.

Longhorn football coaches took one look at Kutner and told him to go play basketball. But he kept begging, and they let him on the team in 1938.

He played in a day with no scholarships. He worked for his room and his food. He swept the floor of the gymnasium and sold "soda water" at basketball and baseball games.

The whole time he worked hard to get bigger and make his 6-foot-2 body stronger. It paid off. By the time he was a senior, this scrawny kid weighed 194 pounds. He was plenty big to play football back then.

He was also really good. An end, Malcolm Kutner and teammate Chal Daniel became the first All-Americas in UT football history. He is a member of the Longhorn Hall of Honor.

Everybody seems to think bigger is better. Bigger houses, bigger burgers, bigger football players. You even super-size your fries. You just can't wait to grow up some so you can be taller and bigger, can you?

But, you know, size didn't matter to Jesus. Salvation came to the house of a bad man who was so short he had to climb a tree to even see Jesus. Zacchaeus was a big shot because he was rich, but that didn't matter to Jesus either. Zacchaeus was saved because he was sorry for all the wrong things he had done, and he changed his life as a result.

The same is true for you. What matters to Jesus is the size of your heart, the one you give to him.

Look at some old pictures of you.
Have you grown much?
Have you grown in your love for Jesus?

DAY 9

CHEERS

Read Matthew 21:6-11.

Some people ran ahead of Jesus, and some followed him. They all shouted.

Once upon a time, there was no "Hook-'em-Horns" sign.

In 1955, a student cheerleader named Harley Clark, Jr., changed cheering forever for Texas fans. A friend of his made some animal shadows on his dorm wall. He extended his index and little fingers and tucked his middle fingers under his thumb. He thought that the shadow looked like a Longhorn. He passed on to Clark the idea that UT needed a hand sign similar to Texas A&M's "gig-em" sign. He showed the cheerleader his creation.

The fired-up Clark tried the Hook-'em-Horns sign on some students. They all thought it was corny. That didn't slow Clark. He showed the

sign at a pep rally before 4,000 students. It caught on at once and was all over the place at the game the next day. To Clark's surprise, the sign never went away.

Hey, you go to school in the morning. You do your homework and your chores. You go to church. You remember to say "Yes, sir" and "Yes, ma'am" — sometimes.

Overall, you're a pretty good kid, but nobody cheers for you. No announcer calls your name. No cheerleader shakes pompoms at you when you pass by.

That's okay. Think what happened to Jesus. A crowd went wild cheering for him when he entered Jerusalem. They threw their clothes on the ground and tore branches off trees. Five days later, the crowd shouted again. Only this time they screamed for Jesus to be killed.

You just remember that you have a personal cheerleader who will never stop pulling for you.

That cheerleader is God.

***Make up a cheer that God
might yell out to support you.***

WINNER'S CIRCLE

Read 1 John 5:1-6.

The person who believes Jesus is the son of God is the real winner in the world.

Here's a win streak so incredible it's hard to believe: The Texas women's basketball team once won 189 straight conference games!

Nobody noticed much when the UT women lost to Texas A&M on Jan. 23, 1978. Back then, papers and TV didn't pay much attention to women's college basketball. The program was in only its fourth season. It was so new that the women had their first-ever game programs that season. They didn't even have a media guide, which is handed out to reporters at the games and tells them about the team.

But that was the last time the Texas women would lose to a team from the Southwest Conference until Feb. 23, 1990. That's when they lost to 25th-ranked Arkansas. The 189-game win streak stretched across an incredible thirteen seasons!

Technically, the streak was 130 SWC games. That's because UT's old league didn't turn the women's game over to the SWC until 1983.

189 or 130 — either way, that's a lot of wins.

Life is a competition; it's not just football or basketball games. You compete against others at school for a good seat in the lunchroom. You try to beat others in a video game.

Competition isn't bad for you as long as you play according to the rules the way that UT's teams do. It makes you stronger.

In everything you do, you should want to win. Winning isn't everything, but you should always try to do your best. Sometimes you will lose, but you don't quit trying.

Only with your faith in Jesus do you never lose. You win — for all time.

Name some things in which you competed and won and some you lost. Did they make you feel different? How?

FAITHFUL LIVES

Read Hebrews 11:1-3, 6.

Without faith, you can't please God.

At Texas, Chris Hall practiced what he preached.

He practiced football. As a senior center in 2009, he was third-team All-America.

But Hall also practiced a way of life. He was and is a man of faith in Jesus Christ. He was a licensed minister while he was at Texas. Football team counselor Brian Davis said Hall was an "absolute, sincere true believer in faith and mankind." In other words, Hall put his absolute faith into practice in his daily life.

Once, Davis was not having a very good day. He was going to have to rip into three football players who had not been behaving themselves. That was never fun.

Angry, he walked out of his office and found the three troublemakers in a circle. Their heads were bowed as Hall led them in prayer.

"I closed the door," Davis said, "went back into my office and said, 'God bless Chris Hall.'"

In your life, you have faith in many things. Faith in people like your parents, your grand-parents, and your teachers. Faith that the Horns will win, that the family car will start, that doing the right thing is the way to live.

This is all great stuff. It makes you a great kid whom everybody likes. Someone people can count on. It makes life fun.

But nothing is as important in your life as what you believe about Jesus. To have faith in Jesus is to believe that he is the Son of God. It is to believe in his words of hope and salvation that are written in the Bible.

True faith in Jesus means more than just believing. You do what Chris Hall does; you live for Jesus. You do everything for Jesus.

Come up with three things you can do tomorrow that will show others your faith in Jesus. Do them.

 DAY 12

JUST PERFECT

Read Matthew 5:43-48.

Jesus said, "Be perfect, just as God is perfect."

Cat Osterman was perfect. The best throw of the game, though, may have been one her catcher made.

Cat is the greatest pitcher in Texas softball history. From 2002-2006, she was a four-time All-America. At UT, she threw twenty no-hitters and ten perfect games. (A no-hitter means no player got a hit; a perfect game means not a single player even reached first base.)

In 2005 against Mississippi State, Cat was closing in on another perfect game. With one out in the seventh and last inning, she struck out one of her 17 batters in the game. The ball got away from catcher Megan Willis. Worried about ruining the perfect game, she said, "I panicked." But she chased the ball down and

threw a strike to first to beat the runner.

She thus saved the perfect game. In fact, Cat was so perfect she didn't need her outfielders. None of them touched a live ball.

To be perfect means you never do anything wrong, you never make a mistake, you never do anything clumsy. Ever.

Oh, you can be perfect now and then like Cat Osterman. On a test. Or playing a song on an instrument. But you're not perfect all the time. Only one person — Jesus — was.

But yet Jesus commands you to be perfect. Didn't we just say that was impossible? Has Jesus got it wrong?

Nope, not at all. When Jesus spoke of being perfect, he talked of loving perfectly as God does. To love perfectly is to love all others and not just those whom you like or who do nice things for you at school or at church.

To love perfectly is to love everyone.

List three folks it's really hard for you to love. Then list something good about each one. Try to love them for that.

AS A RULE

Read Luke 5:27-32.

Some religious leaders complained because Jesus broke the rules and ate with sinners.

Texas head football coach Darrell Royal didn't like the new rule, but he used it to win a game.

Before the 1958 season, the two-point conversion after a touchdown was put into place for the first time. Royal was against the change and he said so. Then when the Horns scored the first touchdown in the '58 Oklahoma game, he went for two.

The coach's decision surprised everyone but his players. On the day before the game, he told his team. He felt that one touchdown would not be good enough to beat Oklahoma.

The Sooners weren't ready for the two-point play. UT guard H.A. Anderson blocked an Oklahoma player so hard his helmet turned around. Fullback Don Allen trotted into the end zone untouched for an 8-0 Texas lead.

Royal's use of the new rule turned out to be the difference in the game. Texas won 15-14, the first game to be decided by a two-point conversion.

You live with a whole set of rules, don't you? Go to bed at a certain time. Don't play in the street. Don't act ugly to your brother or sister. Be polite to your teachers.

Rules are hard but they aren't always bad things. Without them, our whole world and our country would be a mess. Nobody would get along, and people couldn't do stuff together.

The rules Jesus didn't like were those that said some people should be treated badly. He broke them, and he expects you to do it, too. You should never mistreat anybody just because somebody says it's the thing to do.

Jesus loves that person. So should you.

Think of a rule that you don't like.
Why do you think you have it?
What would happen if you broke it?

GOD'S HOUSE

Read 2 Samuel 7:2-7.

*The Lord said, "I have been living
in a tent."*

One Longhorn family has a whole bunch of history with old Gregory Gym.

In 1949, a Texas student walked up to the ticket window in Gregory where his girlfriend worked. He flashed a diamond ring at her and asked, "Do they sell these here?" They were married in 1950.

Their daughter, Debi, attended Texas and worked in that same ticket office. She saw a UT basketball player named Lynn Howden shooting in the gym one day. He really liked playing in the little gym. "We didn't mind diving for loose balls," he said. "You might land in a pretty girl's lap." Debi liked what she saw and flirted with him. It worked.

Their daughter, Bethany Howden, made it three generations with ties to the building.

She played volleyball in the old gym and was a three-time All-Big 12 selection.

When Gregory was renovated, Bethany's mom didn't like that they turned the ticket office into a men's rest room.

Buildings like Gregory Gymnasium have a lot to do with people's lives. Think about the house you live in. Or your school.

But there's another building that should be really important to you: your church. It isn't just a building where people worship.

A church — your church — is actually God's house. God lives there. Long ago, the only place where God could visit his people was in a lousy tent. Now, you go to church looking for God, hoping to find God there.

Whether you find him depends on how hard you look. And if you're looking for him with all your heart and all your love.

List some things you do at your church. Then write down what each one has to do with God.

DAY 15

SMART MOVE

Read 1 Kings 4:29-31; 11:4.

Solomon was wise until he grew old and didn't follow God with all his heart anymore.

UT head football coach Darrell Royal made a smart move his first year in Austin. It had to do with smarts first and football second.

The legendary coach took over as the head Longhorn in 1957. He found that fifteen of his players had grades so bad they couldn't play football. He had enough players to win; he just couldn't get them on the field.

So Coach Royal made a smart move that is routine today for college football programs. He hired a "brain coach," the first academic counselor in college football history.

The hiring signaled that the day of the dumb jock — if it ever existed — was over at Texas. Before long, the grades of the Longhorn football players were higher than the rest of the students.

The next fall, only three of Royal's players couldn't play because of their grades. "It was the best move I ever made," the head coach said. It was certainly a smart move.

Remember that time you left your homework lying on your desk at home? That cold morning you went to school without a jacket? The time your library book was overdue?

Just because we make some good grades in school doesn't mean we don't do some dumb things now and then. Plenty of smart people sometimes say and do things that aren't too smart. Like Solomon when he got old.

Some people even say that if you're really smart you can't believe in God. How dumb is that? Who do they think made us smart in the first place?

You got your brains and your smarts from God. Forgetting that isn't smart at all.

Talk about why it's smart
to love God and follow Jesus.

DAY 16

FIGHT NIGHT

Read Hebrews 12:14-15.

Do all you can to live in peace with everyone.

Mouthing off to Ed "Shipwreck" Kelley during a football game was not a good idea. One North Carolina lineman made that mistake.

Before he played football and basketball for the Horns, Kelley worked at keeping the peace in places where sailors liked to hang out. He would throw troublemakers out into the street.

The 1948 Longhorns went 7-3-1, but they ran into trouble against North Carolina. "They beat us like a drum," said UT back Tom Landry, later the coach of the Dallas Cowboys.

"Shipwreck" didn't take too kindly to the whipping, especially when the guard across the line started talking about it. Finally, he had enough. He hit the kid under the chin with his forearm. "He raised him a good foot off the ground," a teammate said. "I thought Kelley had killed him."

The Carolina player survived, and the UT coach made Shipwreck apologize to the Tar Heels. He did, but he said later he wanted to tell them he hoped they all broke their legs.

Have you ever played in a game of some kind where a player from the other team hurt you? Maybe you wanted to fight because of it, get revenge the way Shipwreck Kelley did.

No matter what happens, no matter where you are, no matter what someone else has done to you — fighting is never the answer. It's not just because you make an enemy. It's also because Jesus said that you should make peace and make a friend instead of fighting.

Making peace often isn't as easy as taking a swing or saying ugly things to someone. It does requires more courage. It's also exactly what Jesus would do.

Is there someone at school you don't get along with? Try talking to that person and making him or her your friend.

DAY 17

STORY TIME

Read Luke 8:36-39.

As Jesus had ordered him to, the man told all over town that Jesus had healed him.

From a massive toilet flush to the pen that ended World War II — the University of Texas has its stories to tell.

Texas Memorial Stadium was updated in the 1990s. The job included work on the stadium's sewer system. Adding some more rest rooms wouldn't help if the water wouldn't flow. That meant new sewer lines.

To test out the new plumbing, folks went to all the rest rooms one day. On cue and at the same time, they flushed all the toilets. Let the record show that the flush flowed.

Jack Chevigny coached UT's football team from 1934-36. After an upset of Notre Dame in 1934, his team gave him a gold pen and pencil set. It read, "To Jack Chevigny, an old

Notre Damer who beat Notre Dame."

The coach was a Marine in World War II and was killed. The Japanese surrender that ended the war took place on the battleship *Missouri*. An American officer noticed the pretty pen being used to sign the papers that ended the war. He asked to see it. It was Chevigny's pen.

Like the Texas Longhorns, you have a story to tell. It's the story of your life. Nobody else in the world has one like it. Part of that story is how you met Jesus. It's the most important chapter of all.

Too many people are shy about talking of Jesus to other people. It's called "witnessing." They say, "I just don't know what to say."

But witnessing is nothing but telling your story. No one can say it isn't true because it is. You just tell your friends or a member of your family the beautiful, awesome story of Jesus and you.

**Tell a parent your story
about how you met Jesus.**

THE HOMEPLACE

Read 2 Corinthians 5:6-9.

*We would really rather be out of
our bodies and at home with God.*

There has never been a baseball field like the Longhorns' Clark Field. It had a hill in it.

The second Clark Field opened in 1928. It was carefully built not to disturb the beautiful land around it. As a result, the field included Billy Goat Hill.

Billy Goat Hill was a cliff that ran from left-center to right-center field. In some places it was 30 feet high! The cliff got its name because the only way to get on it was through a goat path.

Some Longhorn center fielders figured out how to climb the thing and stop fly balls from being home runs. Some even played atop the hill to keep balls in front of them.

One Texas A&M player tried that trick but then couldn't figure out how to get down the hill. The game had to be held up for several minutes while he climbed down.

Billy Goat Hill gave the Longhorn baseball team a big homefield advantage.

When somebody says "home," what do you think about? A house? Your room? Your toys?

But home isn't just a place. More than walls and floors, a home is about people. You are at home when you are with the people you love and the people who love you. That's why it doesn't matter what you live in. What matters is the people you share it with, including God.

Oddly, as a Christian, you spend your whole life as a kid and as a grown-up away from your real home. That's because your real home is with God and Jesus in Heaven. There you will live forever with the people whom you love and who love you most of all.

You'll be home because you'll be with God, and nobody loves you more than God does.

List the different places you have lived.
What was different about each one?
What made them all feel like home?

LESSON LEARNED

Read Psalm 143:8-11.

Teach me what you want me to do because you are my God.

UT's football coaches once rolled around on the ground to teach their players a lesson.

The Longhorns opened the 2004 season by beating North Texas 65-0. The team didn't do too much wrong except for one thing. They fumbled three times.

So at practice the next week for the Arkansas game, head coach Mack Brown gathered his team around him to teach them a valuable lesson. "If somebody throws you a ball, put it away," he said. Then he tossed a football to another coach, who hugged it tightly. The coach then threw the ball back to Brown, who did the same.

The coaches then went one step further. "If somebody drops a ball, get on it," Brown said. He rolled the ball to a coach who dropped to the ground and curled around the ball. He then rolled it back to the head coach, who hit the ground and covered the ball.

Saturday, Texas led Arkansas 22-20 late in the game, but the Hogs were close enough to kick a field goal that would win the game. But they fumbled. Safety Michael Griffin hit the ground, fell on the ball, and tucked it away.

He had learned the lesson and UT had a win.

You learn lessons every day at school. Math, science, language arts. But life outside of school teaches you lessons, too. How to bait a hook. How to dance. How to hit a softball. Good manners. In every case, somebody teaches you.

And you learn lessons about your faith, too. God set down in his book all you need to know about living a godly life. He even sent Jesus to show you how you are to treat other people.

Just like in the classroom, you need to be a good student to learn God's lessons.

What's your favorite subject?
What about it do you like the most?

OF GENTLE MEN

Read John 2:13-16.

Jesus made a whip out of cords and drove the animals and the money changers out of the temple.

Texas coach Jack Gray had promised himself he would behave like a gentleman. But, hey, a bad call is a bad call.

Gray was UT's first basketball All-America. In 1937, two seasons after he played, he was named head coach. He was 25.

Gray took his team to New York City to play in Madison Square Garden. This was 1939 and the Garden was the most important sports arena in the country. It was expected that coaches and players would behave there.

Gray was a gentleman during the game — until the Horns got what he felt was a bad call. Upset, he grabbed a basketball and slammed it to the floor. He knew right away he shouldn't have done that. He refused to watch the ball rise toward the ceiling. "Has it come down yet?" he asked. "No, sir," the team manager answered. "But it's stopped going up."

Gray got a technical foul, but Texas won 54-32. The head coach told the manager to sit by him, keep a finger in his belt, and not let him get up. He would be a perfect gentleman.

A gentleman is a man who is kind, nice, and polite to other people. He isn't mean to others and always tries to do the right thing. Jesus was a gentleman and acted like one.

But as Jesus showed that day in the temple, being a gentleman doesn't mean that you are weak. It means you stand up for what is right. At school, you protect those who are weaker than others, who are being bullied.

God is a gentleman, too. He could bully you and boss you around. Instead, he gently asks for your attention and waits for your answer.

Talk to your dad or granddad about how a gentleman acts. Decide if that is how God wants you to act.

SUPERSTITION

Read 1 Samuel 28:5-8, 11-14.

Saul said, "Find me a woman who can talk to the dead, so I can ask her some questions."

Tired of losing to Texas A&M, some superstitious Texas students once went to a fortune teller for advice.

In 1941, A&M was undefeated and ranked No. 2 in the country when the teams played on Thanksgiving Day. Texas had not beaten A&M on its home field since 1923. Some Texas fans thought the team was jinxed by the field.

So some students went to see Madam Augusta Hipple, an Austin palm reader and fortune teller. She couldn't tell the future, of course, but she knew about motivation. She told the students to burn red candles the week of the game to bring bad luck to the Aggies.

Red candles soon showed up everywhere in Austin. They were in all the windows of student rooms and houses all over town.

The result was that school spirit was at an all-time high. Texas won 23-0 and finished at No. 4 in the country.

Most everybody is at least a little bit superstitious. They'll knock on wood or won't walk under a ladder. A rabbit's foot may be good luck, but if it's on a key chain, it wasn't very lucky for the rabbit.

Have you ever seen one of those signs with a picture of a hand on it? It may say "Palm Reader" (like Madam Hipple). That's sort of the person King Saul went to for advice.

The problem was that God had told Saul not to do that. He tells you the same thing. Why? What's the harm? Well, if you do that, then you are trusting in people and not God.

Even if you're not superstitious, you trust in and rely on something. It should be God — and God alone.

What superstition do you have?
Superstition is silly, so why is it bad?

WHO, ME?

Read Judges 6:12-16.

"Lord," Gideon asked, "how can I save Israel? I'm a nobody even in my own family."

The touchdown that won the 1962 Cotton Bowl for Texas was scored by a player who couldn't believe he got to run the ball.

The fifth-ranked Horns were underdogs to third-ranked Alabama. With only 12:27 left in the game, Alabama led 10-0.

But UT quarterback Robert Brewer scored on a 30-yard run to make it 10-7. After an Alabama punt, the Horns moved to the Tide 8-yard line. Then came a play that was downright shocking, especially to the player whose number was called.

It was a simple play, nothing but a quick fullback run up the middle. The fullback was Terry Orr; his job had always been to block for the team's flashy tailbacks. So when he heard the call, his eyes got wide with disbelief. "I was surprised," he said. "I was just waiting to hear who I was supposed to block."

Orr got the handoff and ran the wrong way — on purpose. He saw a hole behind a perfect block and scored with 2:05 to play. It was the game winner in the Horns' 14-12 upset.

You ever said, "Who, me?" as Terry Orr did? Maybe when the teacher called on you in class? Your stomach kind of knots up, doesn't it? You get real nervous, too.

That's the way Gideon felt when God called on him to lead his people in battle. And you might feel the same way when somebody calls on you to say a prayer. Or to read a part in Sunday school.

Hey, I can't do that, you might say. But you can. God wants you to do stuff for him. Like Gideon, God thinks you can do it just fine. And with God's help, you will. Just like Gideon.

Think of some ways you can help at Sunday school. And then volunteer.

DAY 23

HAVE A HEART

Matthew 6:19-24.

*You can't serve two masters. You
will love one and hate the other.*

The pros threw $24 million at a Longhorn who
once washed windows to get pocket money.
But he went with his heart and not his head.

In 1997, junior running back Ricky Williams
led all of college football in rushing. He finished
fifth in the Heisman Trophy voting.

NFL teams had millions of dollars waiting
for him to turn pro. It was a lot of money for
anyone, but especially for Williams. He had
once worked on Sunday mornings before a
local fast-food place opened. He washed the
windows and scrubbed the floors. He earned
a grand total of $4.95 each time he worked.

The Horns had a bad year in 1997 despite
Williams' great season. He needed the money,
but he didn't want his Longhorn career to end

that way.

So he went to see the new head coach, Mack Brown. He asked him, "Coach, do I do what people tell me to? Or do what my heart tells me to?" The coach told him to do what he really wanted to.

Williams went with his heart and stayed at Texas. He won the Heisman Trophy in 1998.

Sometimes you must make a choice. Some other boys or girls might want you to do something that you know in your heart isn't right. Like cheat on a test or lie to your parents.

Your head says be cool and go along with the crowd. Your heart says it's wrong. How do you decide? Flip a coin? Use a dart board?

Nah. You turn to the one who should be number one in your life: Jesus. You figure out what Jesus would do.

Your head tells you what Jesus wants you to do. Your heart tells you that it is right to do it.

Pretend you're asking Jesus if you should cheat on a test. Make up what you think he would tell you.

DAY 24

NEW STUFF

Read Colossians 3:8-10.

You have started living a new life.

The new UT team in town held its first practice in the fall of 1995. Every one of the players showed up. All four of them.

Their new head coach dubbed them the "Fab Four." They were the first four players to receive a scholarship to play softball at Texas.

The four moved around campus together. Their friends noticed there were only four of them and asked, "Where's your team?" One player said, "They'd kid us — 'They don't have softball here.'"

Before the fall was over, the Fab Four did have some teammates. Sixteen walk-on players joined them in October. That new team didn't have a home that first season. While a new stadium was being built, they played their home games at Austin's youth fields. The first game was played on Feb. 15, 1996, a day one player said "will go down in history."

It didn't take that new team long to get real good. By the third season, the new UT softball team was in the College World Series.

You get new stuff all the time. A new video game, new teachers, new school subjects with their new books. You may get a new brother or sister or a new place to live. You get new toys or clothes (yuck) at Christmas.

All this pretty new stuff doesn't make a new person out of you. Inside, you're the same.

All of us have some things we would like to change about ourselves to make us better. Maybe you need to study harder. Or do your chores faster. Maybe know the Bible better.

You can be a brand new kid, changing so your life is more fun and you do what you're supposed to. A new you is possible through trusting in Jesus, who can make all things new.

Name two things you'd like to change about yourself. Start praying to Jesus, asking for his help in changing you.

DAY 25

TRICK PLAYS

Read Acts 19:11-16.

*Some tricksters tried to use Jesus'
name to drive out evil spirits. They
wound up naked and bleeding.*

Sarah Lancaster got to play a second sport
at Texas because of a trick shot.

From 2007-10, Lancaster was a star on
the UT women's tennis team. As her senior
season wound down, her coach urged her to
try out for the basketball team. Under college
rules, she could play a sport other than tennis
for one year.

Lancaster thought the whole idea was a joke.
She figured she wasn't good enough anyhow.
Her coach thought different. She had seen
Lancaster making trick basketball shots when
rain kept the tennis team from practicing.

One day, Lancaster was fooling around on
the court. She dribbled toward the basket,
took the ball around her waist and under her

left leg, and flipped it through the hoop. A teammate videoed the trick shot.

The basketball coach saw it and asked the tennis star to join the team. She did. In 2010-11, Lancaster played guard in about half of UT's games. All because of a trick shot.

Sometimes simple tricks like Sarah Lancaster's trick shots can be funny. Not all tricks are nice, though; not all tricks are fun. Those that hurt other people or hurt their feelings are not nice tricks to play.

Some people will try to trick you by leading you away from God's word or Jesus. You have to be careful. They may try to trick you by telling you that what Jesus said isn't really true, that he isn't really the Son of God.

It's a funny thing about Jesus. His good news does sound too good to be true: Believe in him and you are saved and will go to Heaven one day. But it's true. It's no trick.

Think about a trick somebody played on you. How did it make you feel?

DAY 26

PAIN RELIEF

Read 2 Corinthians 1:3-7.

*God is the father of all comfort in
our pain and our suffering.*

Jerry Sisemore was hurt bad, but his team
couldn't win without him. So he ignored the
pain and limped back into the game.

Sisemore, an offensive tackle, was a
two-time All-America (in 1971 and 1972). In
one game, a sportswriter said he knocked
down five guys on one play. Nobody believed
it. The game film showed he hadn't blocked
five men after all; it was six.

In the 1972 Baylor game, the score was tied
at 3-3 in the fourth quarter. Texas couldn't
score in part because Sisemore was on the
bench with a sprained ankle. As the last
quarter began, he went to the trainer, pointed
to his ankle, and said, "Tape it."

Then he limped into the game. He had on

a white uniform and so much tape that one writer said he looked like a snowman.

With a hurting Sisemore in the game, Texas drove for two straight touchdowns. They won 17-3, helped out because Jerry Sisemore had the heart and the will to play with pain.

Does a day go by when you don't feel pain? Maybe a scrape from a fall on the playground. A blister from your shoes. A bump on the head.

Some pain isn't just physical. Bruises and bumps don't hurt nearly as bad as it does when someone calls you names or is mean to you at school.

Jesus knows all about pain. After all, they drove nails into his hands and feet, hung him on two pieces of wood, and stuck a spear in his side. It was an awful, painful way to die.

So when you hurt, you can find comfort in Jesus. He's been there before. He knows all about tears and pain.

Look over your body for bumps, bruises, scratches, and scrapes. Tell how you got each one and how bad it hurt.

DAY 27

DEAD WRONG

Read Matthew 26:14-16; 27:1-5.

*Judas was ashamed and sad
because he had betrayed Jesus.*

Talk about wrong! The umps called a runner out at first base — when the ball was in right field! To make it worse, that bonehead call cost the Longhorns a shot at the national title.

In 1969, the Horns took on New York University in the College World Series semifinals. Texas trailed 3-2 with two outs in the top of the ninth. The catcher doubled, and the next batter hit a ball behind first base. That's when everything went wrong.

The NYU first baseman knocked the ball down, got the ball in his glove and dived for the bag. He beat the runner to first base and the ump called him out. The umps headed for the dugouts as the Longhorn catcher crossed home plate. The game was over. Or was it?

Down in the bullpen, a Texas pitcher saw a baseball rolling around in right field. Then the NYU right fielder hurried over and fielded the ball. The first baseman had dropped the ball!

The Texas coach pointed out that the right fielder had the ball, but the umps said nobody had seen it. The dead wrong call stood.

Everybody's wrong at some time or other. Maybe you walked into the wrong classroom at school. How many times have you come up with the wrong answer on a test?

Here's a secret: Even grown-ups are wrong.

Think about Judas. He turned Jesus over to folks who wanted to kill him. Can anything be more wrong than that?

Judas felt sorry about what he did to Jesus, but it didn't help. That's because he tried to make it all right himself instead of asking God to forgive him. He was dead wrong this time.

When you do something wrong, you make it worse if you don't pray to God for forgiveness.

Think of something you did wrong today. Ask God to forgive you. How do you feel?

FEAR FACTOR

Read Matthew 14:25-31.

Jesus said, "Be brave. It is I. Don't be afraid."

Kathleen Nash wasn't afraid of much of anything. Even after she broke her nose in practice, she wouldn't wear a mask in games.

Nash is one of the greatest players in Texas women's basketball history. She finished up in 2011 as the only Texas women's player to score 1,000 points, grab 700 rebounds, and hit 200 three-point shots.

At one stretch in her senior season, she looked like she had gone a couple of rounds with a boxer — and lost. During a practice, a teammate broke her nose with a swinging elbow. That was only a week after she got a black eye in practice.

Fearless, Nash refused to wear a mask in the games. So what happened? Her nose got broken again! After that, she decided to wear a mask for a while.

The black eye healed up fast. Her poor nose, though, stayed black and blue and swollen for the rest of the season. She played right on.

Even the fearless Nash admitted that it had been a tough season.

Most everybody's afraid of snakes and big old hairy spiders. Lots of folks don't like bad weather very much. Or high places.

Over and over in the Bible Jesus tells us not to be afraid. Does this mean not to fear a car that's coming at you? How about a big, slobbery dog that doesn't look too friendly?

Of course not. Fear is a helpful thing God put in you to help keep you safe.

What Jesus is talking about is being afraid of everything. Living in fear all the time. God says don't live like that. Trust in him, be brave, and he will calm your fears.

Think of two things you're afraid of. Are they things you should be afraid of or are they silly fears? Ask God to help you lose the fear of silly stuff.

DAY 29

ANIMAL STORY

Read Psalm 139:1-6, 13-14.

*I praise God because of the
wonderful way you made me.*

Before there was Bevo, there was Pig.

The first living University of Texas longhorn steer mascot showed up in 1916. When World War I broke out, he was forgotten and left on the farm. He wound up as the meal at a dinner honoring the 1920 team!

For a while, Texas had another mascot. It was Pig, a tan and white pit bull mix. He was named after the center on the 1914 team, Gus "Pig" Dittmar. When they stood side by side on the sideline, both were bowlegged.

Pig ran loose on the campus. He often went to classrooms and spent cold days in the UT library. He was present at all athletic events.

On New Year's Day 1923, Pig was struck by a car and died a few days later. Hundreds of people filed by his casket. The Longhorn band led the funeral crowd on the walk to the site where Pig was buried on campus.

The university went without a mascot until 1932 when Bevo II took over. The steer didn't show up at all football games until 1966.

We get a kick out of animals like Pig. Isn't it fun on a trip to spot wild turkeys or deer in the woods? And a zoo is one of the most fun places in the world to visit. Who in the world could dream up a walrus, a moose, a pit bull, or a longhorn steer?

Well, God dreamed them all up, just like he did the possum and the armadillo. And just like he dreamed up you.

You are special. You are one of a kind, a person personally made by God. If you wore a label like the one you have on your shirts, it might say: "Lovingly handmade in Heaven by #1 — God."

***How special does it make you feel to
know that God himself made you?
Share that feeling with your parents.***

WATER POWER

Read Acts 10:44-48.

*Peter asked, "Can anyone keep
these people from being baptized
with water?"*

Colt McCoy and his dad went for a swim — to save a life.

McCoy won more games (45) than any other Texas quarterback in history. As a junior in 2008, he was runner-up for the Heisman.

Memorial Day weekend in 2006, he was relaxing and fishing with his dad. Across the lake, a man who had worked with the first flight to the moon suddenly had a seizure. His wife screamed for help.

Colt and his dad heard her. They decided it was too far around the lake, and they didn't have a boat. They said, "We've got to swim."

So they did. The lake was about 300 yards wide. When they arrived, help was on the way. But somebody had to climb the rocks to the road that lay above the lake. Nobody was in shape to make that climb — except for Colt McCoy.

Without any shoes and with a flashlight, he climbed to the road, flagged down the ambulance, and led the medics to the sick man.

Then Colt and his dad hitched a ride back to the supper that was waiting for them.

Do you like to go swimming? Or take a boat ride? Man, the beach is fun with all that sand, sun, and water. Is anything more exciting than a water slide?

Water is fun, but you need it to stay alive. You have to drink water every day.

Water is so important that it is even a part of your faith in Jesus. It's called baptism. A person who is baptized — including you — is marked by the water as someone who belongs to Jesus. It tells the world you are a Christian and that Jesus is your Lord.

Have you been baptized? If so, talk about what it was like. If not, is it time?

DAY 31

PRETTY MUSIC

Read Psalm 98:4-6.

Shout to the Lord, burst into song,
and make music.

The song all Texas fans know and love got its start as a joke.

In 1902, two UT students set out to create a song special to the university. They wrote a poem and set it to the tune of "I've Been Working on the Railroad." Then they made some changes so it would be a joke on the president of the school, William Prather. The phrase he liked to say to the students was, "Remember, the eyes of Texas are upon you."

Texas students started repeating the phrase to each other as a joke. These were the words the two students used in their new song.

In 1903, at a music show to raise money for the track team, four students sang the song for the first time. It was "The Eyes of Texas." Before the first verse ended, the place had gone wild.

The four students had to sing the song so many times that they got hoarse. The varsity band learned the tune, and the university had a song that still today it calls its own.

Texas fans the world over really like to hear "The Eyes of Texas." They'll get up, sing along, move around, and make noise.

If you like music, then you have music in your heart. But do you ever let that music come out in praise of God the way it comes out in praise of the Longhorns? Do you sing in church, or do you just kind of stand there and mumble a few words? Are you embarrassed to sing?

Music and singing have almost always been a part of worshipping God. Think about this: God loves you and he always will. That should make you sing for joy, especially in church.

Sing your favorite song and your favorite church song. Remember that God likes to hear you sing praises to him.

YOU DECIDE

Read James 1:5-8.

*A person who doubts God can
never decide what to do.*

Texas head coach Darrell Royal had to make
a decision. The national title depended on it.

In the 1970 Cotton Bowl, the Horns trailed
Notre Dame 17-14 with only 2:26 left in the
game. Texas was at the Irish 10, but it was
fourth-and-two.

Royal called a time out to talk over his
decision. Texas could kick a field goal and tie
it. That meant the national title would go to
Penn State or Southern Cal. Or Texas could go
for it, losing the game if they didn't make it.

On the field, wide receiver Cotton Speyrer
looked over the Notre Dame defense. He
signaled his head coach that he would be open
on a pass to the outside. The coach decided;
he called for a pass.

Sure enough, Speyrer was open. The

quarterback hit him with a pass for the first down. Texas scored three plays later and won 21-17.

The Horns were national champs — thanks to a very good decision.

Most of the decisions in your life are made for you, aren't they? Your parents, your grand-parents, your teachers, your coaches — they decide things for you.

So when you do get the chance to make a decision, you don't want to mess it up. How can you make a good decision? It isn't always easy; sometimes deciding what to do is hard. So what do you do?

You talk it over with your parents. You pray about it with them. You look in the Bible with them to see if God has a word about the choice you face. When you know what God's answer is, you do it. When you obey God, you can know that you are doing the right thing.

Make a list of the decisions you will make tomorrow. Go ahead and pray for God's help in making them.

TOP SECRET

Read Romans 2:1-4, 16.

One day, God will appoint Jesus to judge everyone's secret thoughts.

What if you thought you had a big old secret — but it turned out everybody knew it? That's what happened to the Texas football team once.

Before the 1968 season, the Longhorns worked on a newfangled offense they didn't even have a name for. Everything about it was top secret. All practices were closed.

Then at a party the night before the first game, against Houston, one of the Houston radio announcers had a diagram of the new offense! It turned out the secret was no secret at all. The whole Houston team and even some Texas students knew about it.

How had that happened? One UT player told his girlfriend about the new offense. She told her brother — who played for Houston. He told his coaches about Texas' big secret.

To make it worse, a Houston sportswriter gave the offense a name. He told the Longhorn head coach it looked like a chicken pullybone. He suggested the name "wishbone."

The Longhorns went on to win two national championships with that "secret" offense.

You probably have some secrets you keep from certain people. Do you tell your sisters and brothers everything? How about your mom and dad? Maybe there's a girl or a boy at school or at church that you really like but you haven't told anyone.

You can keep some secrets from the world. You must never think, though, that you can keep a secret from God. God knows everything: all your mistakes, all your sins, all the bad things you say or think.

But here's something that's not a secret: No matter what God knows about you, he still loves you. Enough to die for you on a cross.

Does it make you feel good or bad to know that God knows your secrets?

UNEXPECTEDLY!

Read Luke 2:1-7.

Mary gave birth to her first child. It was a boy she named Jesus.

They were called "a third-rate team" that didn't even belong in a bowl. Everybody expected them to get killed in the Orange Bowl. Funny thing about that.

Sportswriters declared the Texas football team of 1948 to be third-rate. After all, they had only a 6-3-1 record. The writers made fun of the Orange Bowl for picking the Longhorns to play Georgia, the champions of the SEC.

The married players didn't even want to go to the bowl game! They didn't want to leave their wives at home over the holidays. The athletic director had to agree to fly the wives to Miami for the game. He also gave the team and the wives a trip to Cuba for a vacation. The players then agreed to play the game.

Still, everybody said they knew what to

expect from the mismatch: a Georgia romp.

Instead, the "third-rate" Horns unexpectedly beat the Bulldogs 41-28.

Something is unexpected when you didn't know it was going to happen — like a Texas win. It can be good or bad. Maybe you had a field trip planned at school and you woke up sick and couldn't go. Or you found a dollar bill on the sidewalk. Life surprises us a lot.

God is just like that. He surprises us so we can remember that he's still around. Like the time he was born as the baby Jesus.

There is nothing that God can't do in your life. The only thing that holds God back is when you don't believe he can do something. Or when you don't live each day with God in your heart and on your mind.

You should always be ready for God to do something unexpected in your life.

Tell about a time you expected one thing and got something completely different. Was it good or bad?

DAY 35

THE GOOD OLD DAYS

Read Psalm 102:1-5.

Lord, my days disappear like smoke.

They wore homemade uniforms and paid for the gas to get to a game. That's the way it was back in the "good old days" of women's basketball at Texas.

In 1966, the PE department agreed to let the coeds play basketball as a nonvarsity club sport. That means it wasn't a real sport.

Eleven players made the first team after tryouts. The game was really different from women's basketball today. Each team had six players; only two of them, called rovers, could cross the midcourt line! The other four played a halfcourt game.

They played in a gym where the court was too small. There weren't even any seats, so nobody could sit and watch the games.

They had to make their own uniforms. When they got some, they had to share them with the volleyball team! They went to games by all piling into a player's car or borrowing a car from a friend. They had to buy the gas and pay for their rooms if they stayed overnight.

When it comes to UT women's basketball, maybe those "good old days" weren't so good.

Women's basketball at Texas isn't like that today because time does not stand still. That means things change. When they do, you have memories, things you remember. Do you remember last year and some of the things you did at school? Remember your baptism? Remember the first time you went zip-lining?

You will always have those memories. God is always with you, too. Today may be one of those good old days you will remember someday, but you must share it with God. A true "good old day" is one God is a part of.

Make a list of things you can do to make God a part of your day (like saying a blessing). Try to do them all.

WEATHERPROOFED

Read Nahum 1:3-5.

*God alone controls the wind and
the storms.*

The Horns and Missouri made history in 1996. So did the weather.

On Aug. 31, the two teams played the first-ever Big-12 football game. It had been the Big Eight Conference since 1957. Ricky Williams ran for 112 yards and two touchdowns to lead the Horns to a 40-10 pasting of the Tigers.

But another kind of history was made that night. In its 72 seasons, Memorial Stadium had never seen a rain delay. This was the first game in the stadium with its new name: Royal-Memorial Stadium. The "Royal" is for legendary coach Darrell Royal. He won more games than any other UT football coach.

As the last half started, winds up to forty miles per hour and nearby lightning greeted the players. Then came a thunderstorm that one writer said made him think of Noah. The storm dumped two inches of rain on the field in 25 minutes, drenching everybody.

Eventually, the refs decided the lightning was too close. They called the teams off the field. The result was the first rain delay in Texas football history. It lasted 45 minutes.

You can look out a window and see a storm coming, but you can't stop it, can you? You can do a lot of things, but only God controls the weather.

God has so much power you can't imagine it. But you also can't imagine how much God loves you. He loves you so much that as Jesus he died in pain on a nasty cross for you.

God is so powerful that he can make it rain and push the clouds around. He even tells the lightning where to go. But the strongest thing of all about God is his love for you.

List all the kinds of bad weather you can think of. Tell a parent what you'd do in case of each one.

DAY 37

BE BRAVE

Read 1 Corinthians 16:13-14.

Stand firm in the faith. Be brave.
Be strong.

On their way to the field before a game, the Texas football players touch a photograph of Freddie Steinmark to remind them to be brave.

Steinmark was a starting safety for Texas in 1968 and '69. During the 1969 season, he found out he had cancer. Less than a week after he played against Arkansas, his leg was amputated.

Within a month, he was back in the Texas locker room for the Cotton Bowl. He was given the game ball after the Longhorns won.

His senior season Steinmark served as an assistant coach for the freshman team. His cancer came back, though. He died in 1971; he was 22 years old, courageous and fighting right to the last day of his life.

He also stood firm in his faith. As he went

in for his surgery, he told his mother, "If God wants my leg, we'll have to give it to Him."

What do you think of when somebody tells you to be brave or have courage? Maybe a firefighter who runs into a burning house to rescue someone? Or a soldier who fights for our country so you can sleep safely at night?

They are brave people, all right, but you, too, show courage every day. Maybe by trying new things or by standing up for yourself with a bully.

God calls you to be brave every day by showing courage for Jesus. You stand firm in your faith no matter what someone else says or does. You show and tell others you believe in God and love Jesus no matter what.

If you do that, then God calls you a hero. Hey, how great is that?

Make a "courage box." Decorate it and put five slips of paper in it with ways you can show courage. Pull one out each day and show courage by doing what it says.

MIDDLE OF NOWHERE

Read Genesis 28:10-16.

*Jacob woke up and said to himself,
"The Lord is in this place, and I
didn't even know it."*

A coach found a great Texas Longhorn player right in the middle of nowhere.

The player was Heather Schreiber. A 6-2 forward, she started every game for the women's basketball team from 2001-05 (133 of them). She was All-Big 12 three times; her name is all over the Texas record book.

The UT basketball coach found her in Windthorst. At the time, 350 people lived there. Some of Screiber's classes at UT were bigger than that. The little town didn't even have a stop light, just one caution light.

So where does a kid go for fun in the middle of nowhere? "The gym," Schreiber said. She led her school, which had 119 students, to four straight state volleyball titles and a berth in the state basketball tournament. She also went outdoors to win the state high jump title.

Schreiber knew about the outdoors. From the fourth grade on, she got out of bed at 3 a.m. every day. She helped milk the family's 100 cows before she went to school and played ball. There in the middle of nowhere.

Did you know there's a town in Texas named Melvin? And one called Rule? There's even one named Old Glory. And another called Guy.

They're little places, not on an interstate highway. They're in the middle of nowhere.

But don't get those towns wrong. They are special and wonderful. That's because God is in Friday and in Electric City, just like he is in Austin, Dallas, and Houston.

As Jacob found out one morning, the middle of nowhere is holy ground — because God is there.

Find some funny names of towns on a Texas map. Remind yourself God is in each one of them.

DAY 39

RUN FOR IT

Read John 20:1-10.

Peter and the other disciple ran to Jesus' tomb.

What made Earl Campbell run? According to Earl, the answer was simple: God did.

Campbell is a UT legend, the school's first Heisman Trophy winner. As a senior in 1977, he led the nation in rushing and points scored. The Horns went 11-0.

Early on, though, the "Tyler Rose" seemed to be running to nowhere. He admitted he was a thug. "I did just about everything there was except get mixed up with drugs," he said.

Still, every Sunday his mama made sure he was in church. One night Earl turned from the streets to God. "I said, 'Lord, lift me up,'" Campbell recalled.

And, oh, how the Lord lifted him up and set him to running. Campbell said his ability was "a gift that God gave me and this is what I am meant to do."

On the sideline during a game, he prepared himself to run again by praying. "I sit on the bench, I put on that [football] suit, and I say a prayer," he said.

You probably do a lot of running. You run at recess and at PE. Spot a playground and you run to it without thinking. You run during a game, whether it's softball or basketball. You run a race to see who's the fastest.

But no matter how hard, how far, or how fast you run, you can never outrun God. He is always there with you. He wants you to run, too — right to Jesus. Life is like a long race, and you win it by running step by step with Jesus all the way.

Here's something odd. The best way to run to Jesus is to drop to your knees — and pray.

Go out and run around your house twice, picturing God running with you all the way.

DAY 40

DYNASTY

Read 2 Samuel 7:12-17.

David's kingdom will never end.

Over the years, Longhorn fans have come to think of their football team as a dynasty, a team that doesn't lose a whole lot. One of the greatest Texas dynasties of them all, however, belongs to the men's basketball team.

The sport began at UT in 1905-06. The team played its earliest games outdoors. Then it rented a local theater for a while. In 1917, the team finally got a home when a wooden gym was opened up.

About that dynasty. The team won its last three games of the 1912-13 season. The squad then went 11-0 in 1913-14, 14-0 in 1914-15, and 12-0 in 1915-16.

During that 1915-16 season, the team beat one team 102-1 and another 80-7. The new, wooden gym, called the "Men's Gym," that opened in 1917 was small, had bad lighting, and didn't have heat. But it was dry.

The Horns won their first four games of the season before losing to Rice. They had won an incredible 44 straight games. That stood as the longest streak in college ball for almost forty years. Today, it is still the fifth longest streak ever. Now *that's* a dynasty!

As much as you want them to, the Horns can't win every Big-12 title or national crown.

Have you ever noticed that your life is like a football season? You win some and lose some. You may be so good at something like a video game or spelling that you almost never lose or make mistakes. But you do sometimes.

Only one dynasty will never end. That's the one God set up with King David a long time ago, even before football. God promised David a king to set up God's kingdom.

That king is Jesus; his kingdom lasts forever.

Name something you're really good at, so good that you're like a dynasty. Then tell about the last time you lost at it.

DAY 41

WHAT YOU WEAR

Read Genesis 37:1-5.

His father made Joseph a pretty coat, and his brothers hated him.

Two students on a date helped lead the way for what Texas' school colors would be.

In 1885, students on a train were headed to a UT baseball game. The custom was to wear colored ribbons to show your team loyalty.

When two coeds said they didn't have any ribbons, their dates went to get them some. A shopkeeper asked them what colors they wanted, and they said, "Anything."

So he sold them white because folks always wanted it for parties and weddings. And he sold them orange because nobody wanted it.

So UT's first baseball team was supported by orange and white ribbons.

Early football teams wore gold and white. Then a change was made to orange and white in 1895. The uniforms were too hard to keep clean, so in 1897, the colors became orange and maroon! They were too ugly to keep.

The students voted and chose to go back to orange and white, like those ribbons back in 1885. They've been UT's colors ever since.

You dress a certain way for school and for church. How silly would it be to wear shoes and a coat into a swimming pool?

Your clothes wear out and you outgrow them. So you change clothes all the time. Getting a new pair of shoes or some new jeans changes the way you look. It doesn't change you, does it? You're still the same person.

Do you think Jesus cares about the clothes you wear? What he cares about is your heart. What he cares about is how you act. It doesn't matter whether you're wearing clothes fit for a king or rags a homeless person might wear.

Clothes don't make you the person you are. Loving Jesus does.

Dress up in a wild outfit. Before a mirror, act out what Jesus would say to you if he saw you.

DAY 42

IN THE KNOW

Read John 4:25-26, 39-42.

"We know that this man really is the Savior of the world."

Texas defensive end Brian Robison just knew. Because he did, he made it possible for the Horns to win the national championship.

On Jan. 4, 2006, Texas played Southern Cal in the Rose Bowl for the national title. The Trojans were only two yards away from winning. It was fourth-and-two at the Texas 45. They led 38-33 with less than three minutes to play.

Robison looked at his teammates and said, "This is it." If the Trojans made the first down, they were the champions.

When Robison settled into his stance, he looked across the line and saw Southern Cal's star running back. He knew what was coming. That back would get the ball.

On the snap, Robison made a surprise move. He went inside and slipped through a hole in the line. Sure enough, the running back came right at him. He grabbed an ankle and held on. Southern Cal was a yard short, and Texas got the ball with a chance to score.

History shows that Vince Young scored the game-winning touchdown with 19 seconds left on the clock. Texas won 41-38.

Brian Robison just knew in the game against USC the same way you know some things in your life. You know what your favorite subject is in school, what your favorite flavor of ice cream is. You know you like the Longhorns.

Nobody can work it out on paper why you know these things. You just do. That's the way it is with your faith in Jesus. You know that he is God's son and is the savior of the world. You know it with all your heart and soul.

You just know it, and because you know him, Jesus knows you. That is all you really need to know.

List ten things you know for sure
about yourself and your life.
Shouldn't #1 be "I am a Christian"?

DAY 43

ANGRY BIRDS

Read James 1:19-20.

*A person's anger doesn't produce
the kind of life God wants.*

The UT women's basketball team was really, really mad. They stayed mad all the way to the national championship.

The Longhorns were ranked No. 1 when the NCAA Tournament began in 1985. They were supposed to win the whole thing.

Instead, Western Kentucky upset them with a shot at the buzzer. "It made us mad," said point guard Kamie Ethridge.

All five starters returned for the 1985-86 season. They were really good. Plus they had an attitude that came out of being mad about not winning the title the year before.

They rode that anger through an undefeated regular season. Guess who they had to play in the Final Four of the championship Tournament. That's right: Western Kentucky.

Still mad, they blasted the Hilltoppers 90-65. They then beat Southern Cal 97-81 to win the national title. With a 34-0 record, the angry Longhorns were the first women's team in NCAA history to go undefeated.

Did you know that getting real mad is really normal? Everybody does it, not just kids. But you have to control it, just like you control the number of sodas you drink.

Think of a time you got so angry you just went wild. What did you say and do? Probably some things you wish you hadn't. Maybe you lost a friend over it. You might have even been punished for acting that way.

God isn't too keen on your getting angry either. That's because it gets in the way of your acting the way you should, the way God wants you to.

So your own anger can make God angry. Making God mad is never a good idea.

Stand in front of a mirror and act like you're real mad about something. Watch how silly it makes you look.

DAY 44

THE PRIZE

Read Philippians 3:10-14.

The heavenly prize is Jesus himself.

A Texas player once won a big award — and he gave it away.

From 1999-2002, Beau Trahan played in 52 football games, mostly on special teams. He was the Special Teams MVP three times.

He also did a lot in Austin. He heard of a 5-year-old named Archer who had a birth defect that kept him from playing with the other kids. He could only sit and watch.

Then one day, Beau showed up at Archer's pre-school. "The little boy who couldn't walk was the hit of the school." When the kids played a game, Archer entered the game riding on Beau's strong shoulders. Beau became Archer's legs. Even when Archer entered kindergarten, Beau stayed in touch with him.

At the 2001 football banquet, Beau's mom

and dad stayed with Archer's folks. They came to see Beau receive the Coca-Cola Community Service Award. It was a big prize, one the players most wanted to win.

Beau didn't keep his trophy long. The next morning, he gave it to Archer.

Hey, we like awards, don't we? A trophy from your baseball or softball team. A certificate for good grades or perfect attendance. A medal for something good you did. Isn't it cool to have your picture in the paper?

We all like other people to notice when we have worked hard and have done a good job.

But you have to be real careful that you don't start worshipping your prizes and bragging about them. That means they become idols.

The greatest prize of all won't rust, fade, or collect dust. It's the only one worth winning. It's eternal life through Jesus Christ.

Rank all the prizes you've won in order of how important they are to you. Compare each one to the prize of being in Heaven with Jesus one day.

GOOD LUCK

Read Acts 1:15-18, 21-26.

They cast lots and Matthias was chosen to be an apostle.

Because he felt lucky, the trainer helped the UT baseball team to a national title.

The 1975 College World Series was down to three teams: Texas, Arizona State, and South Carolina. They all had one loss each. The rules said they had to draw to see which team got the day off while the other two played. It's called a "bye." The team with the bye would then play the winner.

The team trainer went to the head coach and said he felt so lucky he could draw the bye. The coach asked, "Are you sure?" "Yeah, I'm sure," was the answer.

So the two walked to home plate for the drawing. The trainer picked an envelope and opened it. Sure enough, it was the bye! The Longhorns would play for the national title.

After a day off, they beat South Carolina 5-1. The champions had a 56-6 record. They weren't lucky; they were good.

Ever think sometimes that other people have all the luck? Another team beats yours because of a lucky bounce. Somebody else finds coins in a video game at a pizza place.

But there's really no such thing as luck, good or bad. That's because luck means all of life is just chance, that nobody's in charge. That's wrong; God is in charge. Even when the disciples flipped a coin to pick a new guy, they knew God had already made the decision for them.

We don't know why good things happen to bad people. We don't know why bad things happen to you when you're not to blame.

But they're not punishment from God. Just keep on trusting him. After all, he's the one in charge of everything.

Look at a penny, a nickel, a dime, and a quarter. What four-word phrase do they all have in common?

STRANGE BUT TRUE

Read Philippians 2:5-11.

Jesus is God, but he became a servant and died on a cross.

Here's something strange. The woman who got a women's gym built on the Texas campus also got rid of women's basketball.

Texas had a women's basketball team playing other schools as early as 1906. In 1921, Anna Hiss was named director of women's PE. She was a champion of fitness for women. She even started a PE major for the women.

But she was dead set against intercollegiate athletics for women. She saw the danger of pampered athletes and of making games like basketball more important than academics.

So she eliminated the women's basketball program. It became just PE with Texas coeds playing against each other.

She attacked women's basketball in colleges everywhere. She said the game was "unfeminine and dangerous." It was too hard for women to play and would hurt them, she said.

Strangely, in 1931, she headed up the construction of a women's gym. She made sure that the courts in the gym were too small for college basketball games to be played there.

A lot of things about life are strange. Isn't it strange that you can't eat all the sugar you want to? Isn't it strange that you can't play all the time when everybody knows that's what kids are good at?

God's kind of strange, too, isn't he? He's the ruler of all the universe; he can do anything he wants to. And so he let himself be killed by a bunch of men who nailed him to two pieces of wood. Isn't that downright weird?

And why did God do it? That's strange, too. He did it because he loves you so much. In the person of Jesus, God died so you can live, so you can be with him one day in Heaven.

***List five things about God that are
strange (like he never dies).
Tell why they're strange.***

DAY 47

ALIVE AGAIN

Read Matthew 28:1-9.

The angel said, "Jesus is not here. He has risen just like he said he would."

For UT football, a 5-4 season doesn't sound like very much. But it brought the program to life again.

In the 1930s, Texas had four straight losing seasons including a 1-8 fiasco in 1938. In 1939, the Longhorns were 2-1 when they hosted Arkansas, which led 13-7 with thirty seconds left. Disappointed Longhorn fans were leaving Memorial Stadium in droves.

Coach Dana X. Bible told the band to play "The Eyes of Texas," called a timeout, and told his players to stand and listen to the song. Quarterback Johnny Gill then made up a play in the huddle. It was a screen pass that went 67 yards for a touchdown.

Excited Longhorn fans stormed the field. The police had to run them off to kick the extra point. It was good and UT won 14-13.

That upset win and the 5-4 season changed everything. The Texas football program was alive again. It had been resurrected.

A resurrection happens when someone who was dead is alive again. Of course, nobody on the UT teams of the 1930s was really dead. In sports, announcers often speak of a team being resurrected. That means it started winning again after losing for a long time.

Resurrections occur in the Bible, but one stands alone. All others are just resuscitations like when an ambulance crew helps somebody stay alive. The person will still die one day.

But when Jesus was resurrected on the first Easter, he was alive forever. And that's the way it will be for you one day. If you believe that Jesus is your savior, you will live forever.

Name some people you know who are in Heaven. Are you sad they're gone? Are you happy you'll see them in Heaven?

DAY 48

PLAN AHEAD

Read Psalm 33:4-11.

The plans of the Lord stand firm forever.

Head coach Mack Brown had his game plan all worked out. Then he threw it in the garbage can at halftime.

The Horns were the underdogs against Oregon State in the Alamo Bowl of 2012. They needed a fast start; instead, the first quarter was downright awful. The offense didn't make a first down, and the Beavers jumped out to a 10-point lead.

At halftime, Coach Brown told his assistant coaches to forget everything they had planned on doing. They had to start over, make some new plans.

The Horns switched to a no-huddle offense. They scored but Oregon State held onto that 10-point lead. It was 27-17 in the last quarter.

But with the new offensive plan, quarterback David Ash got hot. He threw one touchdown pass to make it 27-24. He completed his last seven passes. The last one was a 36-yard TD chunk to wide receiver Marquise Goodwin.

With the change in plans, the slow-starting, fast-finishing Horns had a 31-27 upset win.

People make plans every single day. You do, too. You plan to go to school. You plan to do your chores. You plan to go spend some time with your grandparents.

But what if something happens to mess up your plans? What if you wake up sick and your plan to go to school doesn't work out? Sometimes even when you make a great plan, it doesn't work out, does it?

God has plans for you, too. God's plan for you has nothing but good things like happiness, love, and kindness. But it will work only if you make God the boss of your life.

What are your plans for tomorrow?
Tomorrow night, think back and see if
they turned out the way you planned.

DAY 49

I TOLD YOU SO

Read Matthew 24:30-35.

Jesus will come on the clouds in power and glory.

Quarterback Vince Young could have said, "I told you so." One of the greatest games in Texas history went just as he said it would.

On Sept. 10, 2005, the Horns played Ohio State. Texas was ranked No. 2; the favored Buckeyes were ranked No. 3. They led 22-16 in the fourth quarter and got a drive going. It looked as though Texas was toast.

Young didn't think so. He met with his fellow offensive players on the sideline. He urged them not to give up and then told them how the game would go. "We've been through this," he said. "Defense is going to get us the ball, and we'll take it play by play."

Sure enough, the defense held, and Ohio State missed a long field goal. Young took the offense on a 67-yard drive play by play. The last one was a 24-yard touchdown pass.

A safety put the final of 25-22 on the board. It happened just as Vince Young said it would.

One day Jesus is going to come back and find everyone who has been faithful to him. He will gather them all up and take them to Heaven. There they will live with God forever in happiness and love. It will be the most glorious time ever.

How do we know that's going to happen? Jesus told us so. When will it happen? Well, he didn't tell us that. He just told us to be ready so we don't miss it.

How do you get ready? It's simple. You just love Jesus. You live your life for Jesus. You remember that Jesus is counting on you, and you do everything for him.

Are you ready?

Put some ice cream in a bowl
and watch it melt to remind you
that Jesus may come back at any time,
maybe even before the ice cream melts.

THE LEADER

Read Matthew 16:13-19.

"You are Peter, a rock on which I will build my church."

Bill Bradley walked around the UT campus with tears in his eyes. He figured his days as a Texas football player were over. So he decided to be a team leader.

In 1966 as a sophomore, Bradley started at quarterback for the Horns. In the third game, he tore his knee up and had surgery. The next season, he was so banged up he said the whole right side of his body was taped up.

Head coach Darrell Royal changed offenses in 1968. The new formation was a disaster for Bradley. In the second game, Royal benched him. Later, he told Bradley he was moving to split end. That's when Bradley figured that he wouldn't get to play much anymore and decided to be a leader who fired the team up.

Then in a game, he blocked a defender so

hard that a defensive coach asked him to move to defensive back. Bradley became a star. His talent and his leadership led the Horns to a 9-1-1 season and a win in the Cotton Bowl. He went on to an All-Pro career in the NFL.

Have you noticed that every part of your life has a leader? Your parents lead the house. Your principal leads the school. Your teacher leads your Sunday school class. Your coach leads your baseball or soccer team.

But here's a wild thought: Are you a leader? You can be, you know. You can be a leader for Jesus. How in the world is that possible?

You don't have to lead by doing things that change the world. You can lead by who you are. You lead by being a Christian, a person who loves Jesus. You live the way God wants you to. Your faith is number one for you.

Others will see you, and they will want to be like you. Like you — the leader.

Volunteer to do something in the church. This will show others you are a leader.

DAY 51

BIG DEAL

Read Ephesians 3:10-12.

*Through the church, God's great
wisdom is made known.*

The plan called for a really big deal: a thrill-
ing game between two powerhouses before
the largest crowd in the history of women's
college basketball. Then the Texas women
showed up.

The Tennessee athletic department cooked
up the idea of a game between two really good
teams. The Horns and the Vols would play on
Dec. 9, 1987, in Knoxville. Tickets were given
away to help set a record for the size of the
crowd. It worked so well that the Tennessee
coach got caught in a five-mile-long traffic
jam. She had to get out of her car and walk
to the arena!

The gym was jammed with 24,563 fans. A
rep from the Guinness World Records Museum
said it was the largest crowd ever to see a

women's college basketball game. It was a big deal. But, as it turned out, "the people were there, but the game didn't quite make it."

That is, the game turned out to be no big deal at all. That's because the Texas women didn't cooperate. Behind Clarissa Davis, they blasted Tennessee 98-78

You've had some big deals in your life. Your baptism, for instance. Some birthday parties. Christmas. Maybe some vacation trips.

And you have some things you probably don't think are big deals. Like eating breakfast and going to school every day.

How about going to church? Is that a big deal for you? Or do you just miss church anytime you can without thinking about it?

The church is a very big deal to God. It is the chief means God uses to work out his plan of salvation for the world. It doesn't get any bigger than that. If the church is a big deal to God, it ought to be a big deal to you.

List five things that are big deals to you. Then tell why they are big deals.

DREAM WORLD

Read Joshua 3:13-17.

*The priests stood on dry ground
in the river until all the people had
crossed into the Promised Land.*

Jack Chevigny's dream was snatched away
from him as it was about to come true. One of
Texas' greatest upset wins was a result.

Knute Rockne picked Chevigny to take over
after him as the head football coach at Notre
Dame. Then Rockne was killed in a plane crash
in 1931. Chevigny's dream of coaching Notre
Dame was about to come true. But Notre
Dame officials decided he was too young for
the job. They hired somebody else.

Chevigny's heart was broken, and he left
Notre Dame. Texas hired him in 1934. And
can you believe it? The second game of his
first season in Austin was against Notre Dame,
which had won 26 games in a row.

Chevigny gave a rousing pregame speech.

He even mentioned his dad, who was about to die and who wanted Texas to whip the school that did his boy wrong.

Texas did just that. The Longhorns won 7-6. Chevigny said it was "a dream come true."

Even at your age, you probably dream about some things in your life. Maybe you think of what you want to be when you grow up. Or you dream about being a football, basketball, or soccer star in high school.

If your dreams are to come true, you must be sure they're good enough for God. He calls you to do great things for him, and no dream is too big for God. The Israelites could only dream of having their own country for a home — until God made it possible.

You must work hard to make your dreams come true. Give them your best. Just make sure God is there with you, and that they're good enough for God to help them come true.

Make a list of your dreams. Talk to your parents about how they can come true.

DAY 53

MAKING UP

Read Matthew 5:23-24.

Go and make peace with anyone you're angry with.

Texas and Texas A&M don't play each other in football anymore because they are in different conferences. Once, though, they quit playing because of a big-time fight at a game.

In 1908, fans and students got into a brawl at halftime. One Texas fan was stabbed three times in the head. After that, things got worse.

Before the 1911 game, officials from both schools said the game would be peaceful with no violence. It wasn't. It was so bad that after Texas won 6-0, the school's athletic chairman cancelled the 2012 game.

The UT football manager accused the A&M head coach of teaching his players "to slug and maim" the other team. After that, the two schools broke off all relationships.

UT's athletic director led an effort to form

a new conference. Texas was willing, but not unless A&M got rid of its football coach. He left before the 1915 season, and the Southwest Conference was born. Texas and A&M played each other every year from 1915-2012.

Part of the fun of college sports and being a Texas fan is making fun of and insulting fans from schools like Oklahoma. It's fun because it's not really serious. As long as the teams play each other, you'll keep digging at folks who are fans of one of the Horns' rivals. You don't ever make peace.

It's different with your friends and family members. When you have a spat with them, you need to make up. You make your own personal peace treaty by saying you're sorry.

Jesus tells us that you are to offer a hand and a hug to a person you've said ugly things to or had a fight with. Saying "I'm sorry" gets you right with that person and right with God.

Think up a time recently when you were ugly to a family member. Tell them you're sorry and offer them a hug.

WHAT A SURPRISE!

Read 1 Thessalonians 5:1-6.

The day Jesus comes back should not catch you by surprise.

Larry Robinson didn't think he was good enough to play big-time basketball. Boy, was he in for a surprise.

Robinson figured he couldn't make it at a college basketball powerhouse. "What I really wanted was a good education," he said. So he chose Texas. At the time, basketball in Austin was struggling. The gym seated only 7,800 people, and there wasn't much money. The Horns just weren't very good.

So Robinson arrived on campus in 1970 and surprised everybody. He rewrote the record books by averaging almost 34 points a game as a freshman!

He was even better the next year. He was the Southwest Conference Player of the Year.

Then a knee injury wiped out most of his junior year. As a senior, he was named the conference's Player of the Year a second time.

To his surprise, Robinson broke all but one of Texas' major scoring and rebounding records.

Is anything much cooler than a surprise birthday party? How much fun would Christmas presents be if they weren't a surprise? Some surprises are about the most fun you can have.

But grown-ups usually spend a lot of time and energy to avoid most surprises. That's because many surprises aren't good things. Avoiding surprises is what adults call planning.

There's one surprise nobody can avoid, however. It's the greatest and most wonderful surprise of all. It's the day Jesus comes back to Earth to take Christians to Heaven.

The Bible tells us you don't know when that will be. It's a surprise. But you can plan for it by loving Jesus and claiming him as your Lord and Savior.

Have you planned for the day Jesus comes back? Tell how you can do that.

COMEBACK KIDS

Read Acts 9:18-22.

Those who heard Paul asked, "Isn't he the one who persecuted and killed Christians in Jerusalem?"

The Texas baseball team once pulled off a comeback so famous that the contest became known in Longhorn lore as "The Game."

On May 10, 1962, Texas and Texas A&M met to decide the conference championship. The winner went on to the College World Series.

A&M jumped all over the Longhorns. It was 9-2 early on. The Aggies led 9-3 when Texas came to bat in the bottom of the eighth inning. After a walk, Buddy New — in the game because the coach wanted him to letter — hit a home run. The Horns added three more runs to trail 9-8 headed into the ninth inning.

The Aggies scored a run to lead 10-8. Then the first two UT batters made outs. So much for a comeback. But a walk, a double, and an infield hit tied the game!

In the bottom of the tenth, New doubled and scored on another hit for the amazing 11-10 comeback win. He was mobbed at the plate as the crowd of Longhorn fans went nuts.

A comeback means you come from behind. You know by now that you don't always win. You make an A on a test one day and sprain your ankle the next. You do all your chores at home but get in trouble for talking in class.

In life, even for a kid, winning isn't about never losing. Things will just go wrong for you sometimes. Winning means you pick yourself up from your defeat and keep going. You make a comeback of your own, just the way Paul and the Longhorns of 1962 did.

Besides, God's grace is always there for you, so your comeback can always be bigger than your setback. With Jesus in your life, it's not how you start that counts; it's how you finish.

Remember a time a team you like made a comeback. Compare that to a time you came back after something went wrong.

DAY 56

PARTY TIME

Read Exodus 14:26-31; 15:19-21.

Miriam took a tambourine. The women followed her and danced.

Bevo was about the only one who didn't go bonkers at a very big Longhorn party.

The cheerleaders, the band, Bevo, a whole bunch of fans, and the football team were in Royal-Texas Memorial Stadium. The scoreboard was lit up.

But the score never changed on this day. It read 41-38 all the time. The players wore jeans, not pads. It wasn't a football game but a party on Jan. 15, 2006. It was a celebration of the national title won in the Rose Bowl by beating Southern California 41-38.

More than 50,000 fans showed up to cheer and party. Before the gates opened up, one family showed up with a 40-foot sub. Others used cell phones to order pizzas.

The crowd whooped and hollered from the

get-go especially when the stadium's jumbo TV showed highlights of the season. The loudest cheer of all came when the team showed up, coming in through smoke.

It was a big party for the national champs.

Man, parties are fun, aren't they? A birthday party with cake and ice cream. A swimming party. Remember that Christmas is a birthday party: It's Jesus' birthday.

It would be nice if life were nothing but one big party. Jesus can do that for you. With him in your heart, every day can be a celebration of the good life.

You will cry; you will hurt. You know that already, don't you? Life is just sad sometimes.

But Jesus lets you find joy in those hurtful times. You live knowing that the part of you where Jesus lives will never hurt.

If you make your life a celebration of Jesus and with Jesus, then the party never stops.

Ask your parents if you can have a small thank-you-Jesus party with three friends. Be sure to say a blessing.

DAY 57

SIGHT UNSEEN

Read 2 Corinthians 5:1-7.

We live by believing, not by seeing.

One of the most famous catches in Texas football history was made by the receiver with his eyes closed.

The Horns were big four-touchdown underdogs to Texas A&M in 1940. The Aggies had won 19 games in a row. "I was scared to death and so was everyone else," said Texas back Noble Doss. "I wouldn't have bet 25 cents on us. They had a machine."

But on the game's first play, all-conference fullback Pete Layden hit Doss with a 32-yard pass completion. Doss knew then he could get behind A&M's defensive backs.

The result was The Catch on the fourth play. It was called "the most famous reception in Longhorn history" for thirty years. Doss made "a twisting, over-the-head catch" to the 1-yard

line. Layden scored on the next play.

The score held up. Texas won 7-0.

A famous photograph showed what UT end Wally Scott claimed right away had happened: Doss made the catch with his eyes closed.

How do you feel about the dark? Most kids don't like it, making up monsters under the bed or in the closet. They're not really there, of course, but the dark sometimes makes us afraid. We like to see things; we like the light.

But seeing things works only for the world around us. It's called the physical world, the one God created for you to live in.

When it comes to God and faith, eyesight is no good at all. We don't "see" God; we don't "see" Jesus. And yet we know God; we know Jesus. That's because we see them through the "eyes" of our faith.

Seeing is believing in the world. Believing is seeing when it comes to God and Jesus.

Close your eyes. What can you see? Call out the things you believe are around you. This is the way faith works.

UNBELIEVABLE!

Read Hebrews 3:12-14.

*Do not have an unbelieving heart
that turns you away from God.*

The score sounds pretty boring: Texas won 3-2. The game itself and what Austin Wood did in it are simply unbelievable.

In 2009, Texas and Boston College played the longest game in college baseball history. It lasted more than seven hours, starting one day and ending after midnight. It went 25 innings, a record. At one stretch, neither team scored a run for 18 innings! The game set all kinds of college records, including strikeouts with 42.

The winning run scored when first baseman Travis Tucker — who set a record with 33 put-outs — singled home Connor Rowe.

Then there's what Wood did. UT head coach Augie Garrido said it was the best pitching performance he had ever seen.

A senior, Wood had never even thrown a complete game (9 innings). In this game, though, he pitched 13 innings. Pitchers *never* pitch that long. But here's what is unbelievable: For twelve and one-third of those innings, he did not give up a hit!

You know, it doesn't really matter if you don't believe in some things. Like magic. Or in a lucky rabbit's foot or dragons.

But it matters a whole lot that you believe in Jesus as the Son of God. Some people say that Jesus was a good man and a good teacher and that's all.

They are wrong, and their unbelief is bad for them. God doesn't fool around with people who don't believe in Jesus as their Savior. He locks them out of Heaven forever.

If you believe, you'll go to Heaven one day and be happy with God and Jesus.

Talk to your parents about some things you don't believe in and some things you do believe in and why.

ON THE MONEY

Read Luke 16:9-13.

You can't serve God and money at the same time.

Today, a player drafted into the NFL gets millions of dollars. As Hugh Wolfe knew, it wasn't always that way.

Wolfe was the first Longhorn player ever taken in the draft. He was one of the greatest athletes of the 1930s. He was a star at Texas in both football and track. He once kicked an onside kick that kept rolling until a teammate fell on it for a touchdown! In that same game, he set a school record with a 95-yard kickoff return for a touchdown.

For students like Wolfe, money was hard to come by. "I don't know how I got by," he said once. "But I managed some way."

He managed by mopping floors and by running errands to pay his room rent. He swept out the UT gym each day for 50 cents an hour.

Wolfe was drafted in 1938, so he got millions of dollars, right? Not hardly. He signed for $4,000. He didn't even read the contract because "that was a lot of money then."

Do you get an allowance or earn money by doing chores like mowing the lawn? Even for kids, a little money is necessary so you can buy some things for yourself.

Folks, especially grown-ups, talk and worry a lot about money. Jesus also had a bunch to say about money, much of it bad.

But money itself isn't evil. Its danger is that some people worship money and not God.

Here's a way for you to decide whether you worship money too much. Do you tithe? That is, do you give ten percent of your money to God, primarily through your church?

God's love must touch your heart and your wallet.

If you don't tithe, why don't you?
Say your reasons to God out loud.
How do you think they make God feel?

BEING DIFFERENT

Read Daniel 3:14-29.

"King, we won't serve your gods or worship your gold statue."

Bobby Dillon was different from all the other football players.

As a senior at Texas in 1951, he was an All-American safety and a team captain. He went to an All-Pro career with Green Bay. He is a member of the Packers, the Longhorn, and the Texas Sports halls of fame.

The first time Dillon touched the ball in a Texas game, he became a fan favorite. In the 1949 season opener, he went into the game as a safety on fourth down. The coaches expected Texas Tech to go for it. But they punted. Dillon caught the punt and went 60 yards for a touchdown. "I was pretty amazed," he said.

So other than being really good, what made Dillon different from other players? When he was 10, he lost his left eye after a series of accidents. Doctors replaced it with an artificial one. So he played with one eye in an era that didn't offer protection for his good eye.

If you're a Christian, then you're different though maybe you don't have a physical handicap like that of Bobby Dillon's. That's because the world wants you to act a certain way while Jesus wants you to act another, different way.

Jesus wants you to worship and be true to God and his Word. Those who don't believe in God or Jesus may make fun of you for living that way. You have to decide. Do you stay with Jesus or do you turn your back on him?

You are different but it's the most wonderful difference of all. As a Christian, you are a child of God. God knows you by name just as your parents do.

The world doesn't like for you to be different. Jesus praises and loves you for it.

With your parents, watch a TV show with a family on it. Find ways they act and talk differently from your family.

GREAT EXPECTATIONS

Read John 1:43-49.

Nathanael asked, "Nazareth! Can anything good come from there?"

Everyone expected Billy "Rooster" Andrews just to be the football team's water boy. He expected more.

Rooster was all of 4'10" tall. With his clothes on, he may have weighed 130 pounds. As expected, he was the Horns' water boy or manager from 1941-45.

But during the 1943 season, the head coach needed a kicker. Rooster figured he could do it. He beat out three other guys for the job. In one game he made two field goals. The other team's coach was really mad; he thought Texas was making fun of his team by using the water boy.

In 1944, Bobby Layne, one of Texas' greatest quarterbacks, joined the team. Rooster and he were roommates and best friends. One night, Layne said Rooster should fake one of his kicks and throw him a pass instead. He did it — twice, throwing two complete passes.

Nobody expected little Rooster Andrews to kick or to throw passes for Texas. But he did.

Everybody expects a lot of stuff from you, don't they? Your parents expect you to mind your manners and behave. They expect you to do your chores, like keep your room clean. They expect you to make good grades.

Your teachers expect you to sit down and be quiet in class. They expect you to do all your class work and your homework.

Have you ever thought that God expects a lot from you, too? Nathanael didn't expect anything good to come from Nazareth, but it did. And God expects something good to come from you, too.

What God expects from you — to live like Jesus — is more important than anything else.

Name some things God expects from you. How are you doing?

 DAY 62

BELIEVE IT!

Read John 3:16-18.

Whoever believes in Jesus will have eternal life.

When the Horns left for the game against Oklahoma State in 2007, every player carried a sheet of paper with "We believe" on it. That belief really got tested.

The Cowboys were coasting 35-14 in the fourth quarter. Texas scored but then wound up at its 1-yard line after a punt. The Longhorns moved to their 25, and then tailback Jamaal Charles ripped off a 75-yard touchdown run. It was 35-28 with 7:30 left. Suddenly, Texas fans began to believe again.

Another Cowboy punt left Texas at its 25. Again the Horns got a big play, a 69-yard pass from Colt McCoy to Jordan Shipley. It was 35-35 and faith was alive and well among the Longhorn fans and players.

The Texas defense held again. McCoy then

led another drive. With two seconds on the clock, Ryan Bailey kicked a 40-yard field goal.

Many shocked OSU fans couldn't believe it. But as writer Bill Little said, "Faith is a strong and powerful thing." The Horns believed — and they had an amazing 38-35 win.

You believe a whole bunch of things without thinking about them much. That the sun will come up tomorrow. That you will have a bed to sleep in tonight. That your parents love you. And you believe Jesus is the Son of God.

But not everybody believes that part about Jesus. In fact, a lot of people, including some in your school, will go around saying that nobody should believe in Jesus.

But they are really, really wrong. You just go right ahead and tell them about Jesus like he told you to. And then, say a prayer for them that they will come to believe as you do.

Make a list of some things you believe.
What if you didn't believe them?
How would your life be different?

DAY 63

HERO WORSHIP

Read 1 Samuel 16:1-13.

Don't judge people by their looks because the Lord looks at their heart.

Some folks see Destine Hooker as a hero because she is one of UT's greatest athletes. Before that, she was a hero because she slapped her father — and helped save his life.

In 2008-09, Hooker was the Big 12 Conference Female Athlete of the Year. She twice was a volleyball All-America. She led the Horns to the NCAA finals in 2009.

She was also a four-time NCAA champion in track and field. In 2006, she helped the Longhorns win the indoor national championship. She remains a true Texas Longhorn hero.

Back when she was 15, Hooker did something even more heroic. She came home one night to find her mother screaming and her father passed out on the floor. Her mother ran to call 911, but Hooker took action. She slapped her father — hard — several times.

He finally opened his eyes and smiled at her. He had gotten dehydrated (his body didn't have enough water).

Isn't a hero somebody — like a firefighter — who does brave or dangerous things to save lives? That leaves you out, doesn't it? You're no hero, are you?"

Well, here's some news. God thinks you're a hero. Every time you help someone, be nice to someone, go to church, say your prayers, tell someone you believe in Jesus — you're being a hero to God.

You see, God's heroes are those who serve him. God's heroes are kids who love Jesus and who would never turn away from him.

God knows whether you're a real hero or not — by what's in your heart.

What makes these people heroes:
firefighters, nurses, soldiers,
kids who are Christians?

DAY 64

REVELATION

Isaiah 53:6-9.

He went like a lamb to the
slaughter and said not a word.

On the bus ride to one of the biggest games in college football history, Texas head coach Darrell Royal showed that he was something of a prophet (someone who says what will happen in the future).

When Texas and Arkansas met in 1969, the Horns were No. 1 and Texas was No. 2. The U.S. president attended the game to present a plaque to the winner saying the team was the national champion.

On the bus, Royal called quarterback James Street up to the front. He told Street that if the Horns fell behind by fourteen points late in the game, they would go for two when they scored. The coach also said which play to run. Street thought it was a joke; no way they would fall that far behind.

They did. Arkansas led 14-0 in the fourth quarter. Street scored, and as Royal had said they would, the Horns went for two and made it. When Texas scored again, the extra point made it 15-14. That was the final score.

The Horns were national champions, thanks to the two-point conversion Royal had seen.

In the Old Testament, you read a lot about God's prophets like Isaiah. Did these guys walk around predicting the future? Not really.

Instead, they delivered a word that God had given them. Sometimes — as when Isaiah spoke of Jesus' suffering and death — that involved the future. But typically, the prophets told the people what God wanted them to do, how God said they should live.

Where is your prophet? How can you find out what God wants you to do? You read the Bible and you pray. It's all right there for you.

Write down five predictions (like your next test grade). Check them later to see how many you got right.

A SECOND CHANCE

Read Acts 9:1-6, 13-15.

God said, "I have chosen Paul to work for me."

Lauren Dickson thought it was all over. Then a bum ankle gave her a second chance.

Dickson was a volleyball star at the University of Virginia. She was from Austin, but the Horns didn't recruit her. She finished up at Virginia in 2009, and college volleyball was over for her. Or so she thought.

But as a sophomore in 2007, she had injured an ankle. She missed the season, which meant she still could play for a year.

She enrolled in graduate school at Texas and figured she might as well give the Horn volleyball coach a call. She thought he might need an extra body at practice. "I didn't think I'd ever play," she said.

But the coach asked her to walk on. She did, and to her surprise, she landed a spot on the team. Not only that, she helped the Horns get to the NCAA Tournament, something her team at Virginia had never done. In fact, they went all the way to the Final Four.

"She's a great story," the UT coach said of Lauren Dickson and her second chance.

Paul was an evil man, persecuting and killing Christians, until he met Jesus. Then his life changed forever. Like Paul, you need a second chance now and then. Like taking a test over. Or getting another at-bat after you've struck out in a softball or baseball game.

Here's something really cool. With God, you always get a second chance. God will never, ever give up on you. He will always give you another chance when you do wrong. Nothing you can do will make God stop loving you.

You just have to go to him and ask for his forgiveness. Then you get a second chance. Every time.

Think about a time you made a mistake.
If you got a second chance,
what would you do differently?

THE SUB

Read Galatians 3:10-14.

Christ took your punishment for your sins upon himself by dying on the cross.

Texas had a chance of beating Oklahoma until the first-string and the second-string quarterbacks got hurt. That left the game in the hands of a sub who hadn't played too much.

Texas was 3-0 and ranked No. 5 in 1977, but next up was Oklahoma. The Sooners were unbeaten, too, and ranked No. 2.

Texas' hopes for an upset took a blow when starting quarterback Mark McBath broke his ankle. Jon Aune came in, which was okay. He had played a lot and had a strong arm. He promptly tripped over a lineman and tore up his knee.

That left only third-stringer Randy McEachern. He had watched the games from the press box the season before. He was telling the radio team who the players were.

So Texas got slaughtered, right? Nope. The sub led the Horns on an 80-yard TD drive for a 13-6 UT win. His teammates carried him off the field on their shoulders. No longer a sub, McEachern started the rest of the season and led Texas to an 11-0 record.

Man, wouldn't life be great if you had a sub to take care of things for you? Like take your tests. Take out the garbage. Brush your teeth.

But did you know that you do have a sub for all matters of life and death? God demands a sacrifice to get us right with him after we sin. A sin is anything that angers God. Once upon a time, that sacrifice meant animals like pigeons and goats. But when was the last time you burned an animal in your church? Why don't you have to do that anymore? How do you stay right with God?

You have a sub in Jesus. He made the sacrifice for all time when he died on the cross.

Describe what would happen if you set fire to a goat in your church.

DAY 67

ON CALL

Read 1 Samuel 3:1-10.

Samuel said, "Speak, Lord. I'm listening."

Every time he got the call, he'd jump up and go out there." So said Texas football head coach Darrell Royal about Large Leo Brooks.

Leo was large for his time. In the late 1960s, he weighed 250 pounds and stood 6-foot-6. He was strong, too. He worked on ranches and in construction during the summer.

He was a back-up offensive lineman in 1968. That changed in the Oklahoma game. With players hurt, a coach asked him to go play defensive tackle. Leo answered the call, and on the first play, he sacked the quarterback. From then on, he played defense.

The next week, against Arkansas, he made seventeen tackles. He was named the conference lineman of the week. But there was something the Texas head coach didn't know. Leo was so sick the whole game that he could hardly breathe.

As always, though, Large Leo answered the call. He did what was needed.

You may have answered the call when a coach needed you to play a new position in a game. Or when your teacher called on you to answer a question.

Did you know God, too, is calling you? God wants you to do something for him with your life. That sounds scary, doesn't it?

But answering God's call doesn't mean you have to be a preacher. Or be a missionary in some way-off place where they never heard of fried chicken, video games, or the Longhorns.

God calls you to serve him right where you are. At school. At home. On the playground. You answer God's call when you do everything for his glory and not your own.

Talk and pray with your parents about the call God might be placing on your life and how you can answer it.

THE PIONEER SPIRIT

Read Luke 5:4-11.

*They pulled their boats on shore
and left everything to follow Jesus.*

Imagine starting a sport no one on the team had ever done before! Heck, one team member played the flute in high school and had never done anything athletic. Yet, they were the pioneers, the first ones.

Texas started a women's rowing program in 1998. The new coach put up flyers around campus to find some team members. She also walked around campus, hunting some coeds who looked like athletes.

She found Kate Ronkainen, who had been a basketball player in high school. "I didn't even know what rowing was, but I thought, 'That sounds cool,'" she said. Mary Beth Goodknight had played the flute in high school, but no sports. She heard about the team from a customer in the store where she worked. She tried out and made the team also!

They were among the pioneers, the first UT rowers. They started a program that won four straight Big 12 titles from 2009-2012 and league championships in 2015 and 2016.

A pioneer is a person, like those rowers, who is the first one to do something or to try something no one else has done before. The disciples who gave up fishing to follow Jesus were pioneers.

Being a pioneer is scary, but it's also fun. Learning something new in school, going to a new place on vacation, riding a new ride at the fair — it's exciting!

God wants you to go to new places and to try new things for him. He wants you to follow him no matter what. After a while, you get really good at being a Christian and then you can help others become pioneers for Jesus.

On a note card, list some things you can do for God. Decorate it and carry it with you all day as a reminder.

DAY 69

TOUGH AS NAILS

Read 2 Corinthians 11:23-28.

*Besides everything else, every day
I worry about the churches.*

Hub Bechtol was so tough he once played a football game with a broken jaw.

An end who played both ways in the mid-1940s, Bechtol was Texas' first three-time All-America. In the 34-7 blowout of SMU in 1944, he showed how tough he was.

Bechtol knocked SMU's best back out of the game with a tackle. The blow was so hard that it left him dazed, too. "I hit him right on his knee with my jaw," Bechtol said.

The star was hurting but played right on despite the pain. After the game, he realized something was wrong. "I picked up a potato chip," he said, "and I couldn't even crack it." Imagine not being able to chew a chip!

His jaw was broken in two places. He had

it wired shut. His sweetheart brought him a chocolate cake in the hospital. Texas' tough football player said he stuffed the cake between the open places in his mouth left by the broken jaw.

You don't have to be a UT football player to be tough, do you? It's tough to get up every morning and get to school on time. It's tough to get all your homework done.

It's also tough to be faithful. Nobody today will beat you for believing in Jesus as they did Paul. But some people you meet — maybe your classmates — may make fun of you for being a Christian. Or they will do things that are wrong and want you to do them, too.

You have to be tough every day to live the way God wants you to. You stay spiritually fit every day by reading your Bible, praying, and helping and loving others. Living that way every day makes you tough in God's eyes.

Promise God you'll stay tough all month by reading your Bible, praying, and helping someone else every day. Do it.

YOU NEVER KNOW

Read Exodus 3:7-12.

Moses asked God, "Who am I to go before Pharaoh?" God answered, "I will be with you."

You never know what a young man can do when he puts on a Longhorn football uniform. For instance, a walk-on made two plays that changed the course of Texas football history.

Tom Campbell was a walk-on even though he had a scholarship. Back in 1965, schools like Texas could give as many scholarships as they wanted. So the head coach told assistant coach Mike Campbell his sons could have the last two scholarships.

There was no big TV announcement. Daddy Campbell simply walked into the boys' room while they were studying and told them they were playing football for Texas. Tom figured he'd wind up holding the blocking dummies so the real players could practice.

But he wound up as a starting linebacker. His interception wrapped up 1969's 15-14 win over Arkansas in the "Game of the Century."

Another Campbell interception clinched the 21-17 win over Notre Dame in the 1970 Cotton Bowl. It also clinched UT's national title.

You're like Tom Campbell and Moses. You never know what you can do until you try. You may think you can't play football, cook supper, or run the lawn mower. But have you tried?

Your parents sometimes tell you to do things you think you can't do. God is the same way. You just never know what God is going to ask you to do. Sing a solo in church. Tell someone else about Jesus. Help an old person.

You may think, "I can't do that." But if it's something God wants you to do, you can. You just have to trust him. With God's help, you can do it.

Think of something you've never tried before but would like to. Decide to do it and pray for God to help you.

NOTES

(by devotion number)

1 Three Texas students who . . . Texas would never trail.: John Maher & Kirk Bohls, *Long Live the Longhorns* (New York City: St. Martin's Press, 1993), pp. 3-4

2 After J. Brent Cox . . . to start the dogpile.: Cedric Golden, "Six Flags of Texas," *Austin American-Statesman*, June 27, 2005.

2 UT catcher Todd Gilfillan . . . about the whole thing.: Cedric Golden, "National Champions 2005 Texas Longhorns," *Austin American-Statesman*, June 28, 2005.

3 Wilkinson broke a foot . . . her to train harder.: "Longhorn Hall of Honor: Laura Wilkinson," *TexasSports.com*, Nov. 17, 2009, http://www.texassports.com/genrel/111709aab.html.

3 She was in first . . . Bible verse (Phil.4:13),: "Laura Wilkinson — Do It for Hilary," http://www.sports.jrank.org.pages/5303/Wilkinson-Laura-Do-Hilary.html.

4 "one of the most . . . Longhorns football.": Bill Little, "Bill Little Commentary: Momma's Roses," TexasSports.com, Aug. 3, 2009, http://www.texassports.com/sports/m-footbl/spec-rel/080309aab.html.

4 She stood in the . . . was not for sale.: Bill Little, *Stadium Stories: Texas Longhorns* (Guilford, Conn.: The Globe Pequot Press, 2005), p. 114.

4 The stress finally made . . . you tell them that.": Little, "Momma's Roses."

5 McCoy was sure there . . . to his kicker:: Suzanne Halliburton "Ain't That a Kick," *Austin American Statesman*, Dec. 6, 2009, p. C01.

6 Layne threw a bad . . . thrown the ball either.": Bill Little, "Bill Little Commentary: The Quarterback's Tale," *TexasSports.com*, Nov. 1, 2007, http://www.texassports.com/sports/m-footbl/spec-rel/110107aad.html.

7 During the game, he . . . look real good.": Steve Richardson, *Tales from the Texas Longhorns* (Champaign, Ill.: Sports Publishing L.L.C., 2003), p. 109.

8 Longhorn football coaches took . . . weighed 194 pounds.: Suzanne Halliburton, "Scrawny Kid, Hefty Hopes," *Austin American-Statesman*, Nov. 11, 1991, p. D1.

9 In 1955, a student . . . never went away.: Maher and Bohls, pp. 131-32.

11 Football team counselor Brian . . . 'God bless Chris Hall.'": Kirk Bohls, "His Strong Faith Carries Hall," *Austin American-Statesman*, Oct. 28, 2007, p. C01.

12 Worried about ruining . . . "I panicked.": Olin Buchanan, "She's Purrfect," *The Austin American-Statesman*, May 22, 2005.

12 she didn't need her . . . touched a live ball.: Buchanan, "She's Purrfect."

13 Royal was against the . . . walked in untouched: Bill Little, "Bill Little Commentary: When the Shouting Has Gone," *TexasSports.com*, Oct 10, 2008, http:// www.texassports.com/sports/m-footbal/spec-rel/101008aab.html.

14 In 1949, a Texas . . . and flirted with him.: Mark Rosner, "Gregory Has Been Good to Howdens," *Austin American-Statesman*, Sept. 1, 2004.

14 When Gregory was renovated . . . a men's rest room.: Rosner, "Gregory Has Been Good to Howdens."

15 He found that fifteen . . . move I ever made,": Roy Terrell, "Kickoff in Dixie," *Sports Illustrated*, Sept. 29, 1958, http://www.sportsillustrated.cnn.com/vault/article/magazine/MAG1002884/index.htm.

16 Before he played . . . all broke their legs.: Mahler and Bohls, p. 199.

17 The job included work . . . the flush flowed.: Little, *Stadium Stories*, p. 32.

17 After an upset . . . who beat Notre Dame.": Little, *Stadium Stories*, p. 28.

17 An American officer . . . It was Chevigny's pen.: Little, *Stadium Stories*, p. 30.

18 Billy Goat Hill was a . . . while he climbed down.: "Before There was a

Longhorn," *Burnt Orange Living*, March 22, 2010, http://www.burntorange-living. wordpress.com/tag/texas-baseball.
   19   "If somebody throws you . . . and covered the ball.: Bill Little, "Bill Little Commentary: The Learning Curve," *TexasSports.com*, Sept. 13, 2004, http://www.texassports.com/sports-m-footbl/spec-rel/091304aab.html.
   20   Gray was indeed a . . . not let him get up.: Bill Little, *Hoop Tales* (Guilford, Conn.: The Globe Pequot Press, 2008), pp. 23, 25, 27.
   21   Some Texas fans thought . . . houses all over town.: Jim Nicar, "The Rose Bowl That Was (Almost) in Austin," *utexas.edu*, Dec. 21, 2009, http://www.utexas.edu/now/2009/12/21/rose_bowl_almost/.
   22   when he heard the . . . behind a perfect block: Pat Putnam, "A Little Texas Ingenuity," *Sports Illustrated Presents Texas Longhorns Football* (New York City: Time Inc. Home Entertainment, 2009), p. 35.
   23   He had once worked . . . each time he worked. Kirk Bohls, "Good Fella," *Echoes of Texas Football*, ed. Ken Samelson (Chicago: Triumph Books, 2006), p. 69.
   23   "Coach, do I do . . . he really wanted to.: Little, *Stadium Stories*, p. 122.
   24   Every one of the . . . go down in history.": Mark Wangrin, "Texas' Softball Dream," *Austin American Statesman*, Feb. 15, 1996, p. D2.
   25   As her senior season . . . to join the team.: Natalie England, "Texas Student-Athlete Spotlight: Sarah Lancaster," *Big12Sports.com*, Jan. 6, 2011, http://www.big12sports.com/ViewArticle.dbml?DB_OEM_ID=10410.
   26   a sportswriter said he had . . . like a snowman.: Bill Little, "Bill Little Commentary: Honoring a Champion," *TexasSports.com*, May 7, 2002, http://www.texassports.com/sports/m-footbl/spec-rel/050702aab.html.
   27   The NYU first baseman . . . wrong call stood.: Wilbur Evans and Bill Little, *Texas Longhorn Baseball* (Huntsville, AL: The Strode Publishers, 1983), pp. 321-22.
   28   At one point in . . . rest of the season.: Rick Cantu, "Kathleen Nash Known for toughness," *The Austin American-Statesman*, March 1, 2011.
   29   When World War I . . . honoring the 1920 team.: Richardson, pp. 7-8.
   29   He was Pig, a . . . buried on campus.: "Before There was a Longhorn," *Burnt Orange Living*, March 22, 2010, http://burntorangeliving.wordpress.com/tag/texas-baseball.
   29   The university went . . . games until 1966.: Richardson, p. 8.
   30   Memorial Day weekend in . . . was waiting on them.: Bill Little, "Bill Little Commentary: Colt McCoy," *TexasFootball.com*, June 8, 2006, http://www.mackbrown-texasfootball.com/sports-m-footbl/spec-rel/060806aaa,html.
   31   In 1902, two UT . . . band learned the tune.: Jim Nicar, "The Origins of 'The Eyes of Texas,'" *Longhorn Band/University of Texas at Austin: History of School and Fight Songs*, http://mbe187.music.etexas.edu/Longhornsband/.
   32   On the field, wide receiver . . . pass to the outside.: Dan Jenkins, "A Gamble in the Closing Moments," *Sports Illustrated Presents Texas Longhorns Football* (New York City: Time, Inc. Home Entertainment, 2009), p. 33.
   33   Before the 1968 season . . . He told his coaches: Richardson, p. 63.
   33   a Houston sportswriter . . . suggested the name "wishbone.": Little, *Stadium Stories*, p. 100.
   34   Sportswriters declared the . . . to play the game.: Maher and Bohls, p. 120.
   35   In 1966, the PE . . . if they stayed overnight.: Richard Pennington, *Longhorn Hoops: The History of Texas Basketball* (Austin: University of Texas Press, 1998), pp. 274-75.
   36   As the last half started, . . . it lasted 45 minutes.: Mark Wangrin, "It Pours, and Texas Reigns," *Austin American-Statesman*, Sept. 1, 1996, p. C1.
   37   During the 1969 season, . . . give it to Him.": Maher and Bohls, p. 176.
   38   Its population at the time . . . "The gym," Schreiber said.: Kirk Bohls, "Horns Harvest Bountiful Scorer," *Austin American-Statesman*, Jan. 14, 2002.
   38   her school, which had 119 students,: Olin Buchan, "Schreiber's Performance

Leaves No Doubt," *Austin American-Statesman*, Jan. 6, 2002.

38   From the fourth . . . and played ball.: Bohls, Horns Harvest Bountiful Scorer."

39   He admitted he was a . . . 'Lord, lift me up,'": Bruce Newman, "Just Born to Be   Great," *Sports Illustrated Presents Texas Longhorns Football* (New York City: Time Inc Home Entertainment, 2009), p. 56.

39   "a gift that God . . . I say a prayer,": Little, *Stadium Stories*, p. 117.

40   The team played . . . games outdoors.: Little, *Hoop Tales*, p. 5.

40   Then it rented a local theater for a while.: Little, *Hoop Tales*, p. 3.

40   called "the Men's . . didn't have heat.: Little, *Hoop Tales*, p. 13.

41   In 1885, students on . . . ribbons back in 1885.: Jim Nicar, "University of Texas Traditions: Burnt Orange and White," *TexasSports.com*, http://www.texassports.com/trads/burnt-Orange-white.html.

42   "Robins looked at his . . . and held on.: "Kevin Robbins, "Young Was the Hero," *Austin American-Statesman*, Dec. 31, 2009.

43   "It made us mad,": Greg Garber, "Seniors, Anger Fuel First Perfect Season," *ESPN.com*, Feb. 28, 2009, http://sports.espn.go.com/ncw/news/story?page=garber_perfect_texas.

44   He heard of a . . . he gave it to Archer.: Bill Little, "Bill Little Com-mentary: A   Touch   of   Class,"   *TexasSports.com*,   Dec.   17,   2001, http://www.texassports.com/sports/m-footbl/spec-rel/121701aaa.html.

45   The team trainer . . . it was the bye! Evans and Little, pp. 351-352.

46   Texas had a women's to be played there.: Pennington, pp. 270-72

47   Disappointed Longhorn fans . . . Stadium in droves.: Little, *Stadium Stories*, p. 41.

47   Coach Dana X. Bible . . . listen to the song.: Maher and Bohls, p. 98.

47   Quarterback Johnny Gill made . . . kick the extra point.: Little, *Stadium Stories*, pp. 41-42.

48   At halftime, the head . . . a no-huddle offense.: Mike Fingers, "Comeback Hooked for UT in Alamo Bowl," *San Antonio Express-News*, Dec. 29, 2012, htttp://www.mysanantonio.com/sports/alamo_bowl/article/Comeback.

49   He met with his . . . take it play by play.": Austin Murphy, "With a   Stunning   Comeback   Victory,"   *Sports   Illustrated   Presents   Texas Longhorns Football* (New York City: Time Inc. Home Enter-tainment, 2009), p. 41.

50   he was so . . . to defensive back.: Maher and Bohls, pp. 163-67.

51   The Tennessee athletic department . . . didn't quite make it.": Hank Hersch, "A Texas Waltz in Tennessee," *Sports Illustrated*, Dec. 21, 1987, http://sportsilllustrated.cnn.com/vault/article/magazine/MAG1066871/index.htm.

52   Knute Rockne picked . . . coach at Notre Dame. Gene Schoor, *100 Years of Texas Longhorn Football* (Dallas: Taylor Publishing Company, 1993), p. 1.

52   Notre Dame officials decided he was too young for the job.: Bobby Hawthorne, *Longhorn Football: An Illustrated History* (Austin: University of Texas Press, 2007), p. 23.

52   Chevigny's heart was broken,: Schoor, p. 2.

52   He even mentioned his . . . did his boy wrong.: Hawthorne p. 23.

53   In 1908, fans and . . . in the head.: Maher and Bohls, pp. 28-29.3   Before the 1911 game, . . . broke all relationships.: Maher and Bohls, p. 35.

53   UT's athletic director wanted . . . Southwest Conference was born.: Maher and Bohls, p. 41.

54   Robinson figured he . . . was a good education,": Little, *Hoop Tales*, p. 72.

54   The gym seated only . . . there wasn't much money.: Little, *Hoop Tales*, pp. 74-75.

55   in the game because the coach wanted him to letter: Evans and Little, p. 281.

56   The cheerleaders, the band . . . coming in through smoke.: Asher Price, "Texas   Longhorns: National Champions, Party!" *Austin American-Statesman*, Jan. 16, 2006.

57   "I was scared to death . . . behind A&M's defensive backs.: Maher and Bohls, p. 99.

57   "the most famous reception . . . for thirty years.: Maher and Bohls, p. 98.

57   "a twisting, over-the-head catch": Bill Little, *Texas Football: Yesterday & Today* (Lincolnwood, Ill.: West Side Publishing, 2009), p. 29.

57   A famous photograph showed . . . with his eyes closed.: Maher and Bohls, p. 98.

58   Augie Garrido said it . . . he had ever seen.: Cedric Golden, "It Was So Long," *Austin American-Statesman*, June 1, 2009, p. A01.

59   "I don't know how . . . 50 cents an hour.: Bill Little, "Bill Little Commentary: Hugh Wolfe — The First of Many," *TexasSports.com*, April 26, 2007, http://www.texassports.com/sports/m-footbl/spec-rel/042607aab.html.

59   He signed for $4,000. . . . a lot of money, then.": Little, "Hugh Wolfe — The First of Many."

60   "I was pretty amazed,": Suzanne Halliburton, "Many Happy Returns," *Austin American-Statesman*, Oct. 29, 1991, p. D1.

60   When he was 10, . . . for his good eye.: Halliburton, "Many Happy Returns."

61   Rooster was all of 4'10" . . . throwing two complete passes.: Brad Townsend, "How a 5-Foot Waterboy at Texas Became a Football Icon," *The Dallas Morning News*, July 22, 2001, http://www.dallasnews.com/sharedcontent/dws/spt/colleges/texas/stories/012208.

62   When the Horns left . . . "We believe" on the front.:Bill Little, "Bill Little Commentary: Visions of the Fall," *TexasSports.com*. Nov. 4, 2007, http://www.texassports.com/sports/m-footbl/spec-rel/110407aad.html.

62   "Faith is a strong and powerful thing.": Little, "Visions of the Fall."

63   Back when she was 15, . . . had gotten dehydrated.: Alan Trubow, "In Good Hands," *Austin American-Statesman*, Dec. 19, 2009.

64   On the busy, . . . fall that far behind.: Little, *Stadium Stories*, p. 103.

65   Texas didn't recruit her.: Mark Swanson, Final Four Is Better," *Austin American-Statesman*, Dec. 16, 2010, p. C01.

65   She figured she might . . . think I'd ever play,": Swanson, "Final Four Is Better."

65   "She's quite a story,": Swanson, "Final Four Is Better."

66   He had watched the . . . the players were.: Maher and Bohls, p. 195.

66   His teammates carried him off the field on their shoulders.: Richardson, p. 93.

67   Every time he got . . . and go out there.": Bill Little, "Bill Little Commentary: Large Leo Leaves Too Soon," *TexasSports.com*. April 6, 2002, http://www.texassports.com/sports/m-footbl/spec-rel/050702aab.html.

67   He worked on ranches . . . during the summer.: Little, "Large Leo Leaves Too Soon."
67   Leo was so sick . . . he could hardly breathe.: Little, "Large Leo Leaves Too Soon."
68   The new coach put . . . the team also!: Pamela LaBlanc, "Launching a New Sport," *Austin American-Statesman*, May 1, 2002.
69   Bechtol knocked BMU's . . . by the broken jaw.: Maher and Bohls, p. 109.
70   two plays that changed the course of Texas football history.: "Tom Campbell Profile," *TexasSports.com*, http://www.texassports.com/genrel/campbell_tom00.html.
70 the head coach told . . . real players could practice.: Suzanne Halli burton, "Campbell's Memories of Irish at Fore This Week," *Austin American-Statesman*, Sept. 18, 1995, p. D1.

Longhorns

Daily
Devotions
for
Die-Hard
Kids

www.ingramcontent.com/pod-product-compliance
Lightning Source LLC
Chambersburg PA
CBHW070122100426
42744CB00010B/1897